SPEARHEA

101st AIRBORNE
IN VIETNAM
The 'Screaming Eagles'

SPEARHEAD

101st AIRBORNE IN VIETNAM
The 'Screaming Eagles'

Michael Sharpe
and Simon Dunstan

Ian Allan PUBLISHING

Abbreviations

AIT	advanced infantry training	H&HC	headquarters and headquarters company	NVA	North Vietnamese Army
AO	area of operation	HEAT	high-explosive anti-tank	PAVN	People's Army of Vietnam
ARA	aerial rocket artillery			PF	Popular Forces
ARVN	Army of the Republic of Vietnam	IED	improvised explosive devices	Pfc	Private first class
ASHB	Assault Support Helicopter Battalion	KBA	killed by artillery	PT	physical training
		KIA	killed in action	RPG	rocket-propelled grenade
BAC	Basic Airborne Course	LAW	light anti-armour weapon	RTO	radio telephone operator
		LCE	load carrying equipment	Sfc	Sergeant first class
CIDG	Civil Irregular Defense Group	LDA	lateral drift (while parachuting)	SLT	swing landing trainer
				Sp4c	Specialist Fourth Class
CP	command post	LFT	light fire team	SSI	shoulder sleeve insignia
		LRRP	long-range reconnaissance patrol	USARV	US Army Vietnam
DMZ	demilitarised zone			USMC	US Marine Corps
DUI	distinctive unit insignia	LZ	landing zone	VC	Viet Cong
FB	fire base	MACV	Military Assistance Command Vietnam	WIA	wounded in action
FSB	fire support base	MIA	missing in action		

Acknowledgements
Photographs: US Army, US Signal Corps, and National Archives via Melinda Day and Simon Dunstan
Design: Compendium Design
Maps: Mark Franklin

Note: Internet site information provided in the Reference section was correct when provided by the author. The publisher can accept no responsibility for this information becoming incorrect.

Previous page: Classic airmobility – an 81mm mortar crew of Company D, 1st Battalion, 501st Infantry (Airmobile), 2nd Brigade, 101st Airborne Division (Airmobile), disembarks from a UH-1H during an operation west of Tam Ky on 1 June 1969.

First published 2005

ISBN 0 7110 3063 4

Published by Ian Allan Ltd

an imprint of Ian Allan Publishing Ltd, Hersham, Surrey KT12 4RG
Printed by Ian Allan Printing Ltd, Hersham, Surrey KT12 4RG

Code: 0505/C

British Library Cataloguing in Publication Data
A CIP catalogue record for this book is available from the British Library

CONTENTS

Glossary

A company is typically the smallest army element to be given a designation and affiliation with higher headquarters at battalion and brigade level. This alphanumeric and branch designation causes an 'element' to become a 'unit'.

Squad: 9–10 soldiers. Typically commanded by a sergeant or staff sergeant, a squad or section is the smallest element in the army structure, and its size is dependent on its function.

Platoon: 16–44 soldiers. A platoon is led by a lieutenant with an NCO as second in command, and consists of two to four squads or sections.

Company: 62–190 soldiers. Three to five platoons form a company, which is commanded by a captain with a first sergeant as the commander's principal NCO assistant. An artillery unit of equivalent size is called a battery, and a comparable armoured or air cavalry unit

is called a troop. During the Vietnam era the 2nd Battalion 327th Infantry consisted of four companies designated H&HC, A, B and C. But in the spring of 1968 two additional companies, D and E were added, revising H&HC's responsibilities.

Battalion: 300–1,000 soldiers. Four to six companies make up a battalion, which is normally commanded by a lieutenant colonel with a command sergeant major as principal NCO assistant. A battalion is capable of independent operations of limited duration and scope. An armoured or air cavalry unit of equivalent size is called a squadron.

Brigade: 3,000–5,000 solders. A brigade headquarters commands the tactical operation of two to five organic or attached combat battalions. Normally commanded by a colonel with a command sergeant major as senior NCO, brigades are employed on independent

or semi-independent operations. Armoured cavalry, Ranger and Special Forces units this size are categorised as regiments or groups.

Division: 10,000–15,000 soldiers. Usually consisting of three brigade-sized elements and commanded by a major general, divisions are numbered and assigned missions based on their structures. The division performs major tactical operations for the corps and can conduct sustained battles and engagements.

Corps: 20,000–45,000 soldiers. Two to five divisions constitute a corps, which is typically commanded by a lieutenant general. As the deployable level of command required to synchronise and sustain combat operations, the corps provides the framework for multi-national operations.

Note: In unit designations the American spelling of armour (armor) is used.

ORIGINS & HISTORY

The story of the 101st Airborne Division – the celebrated 'Screaming Eagles' – stretches back over more than half a century of war and peace. Since its inception at Fort Bragg in 1942, through the tough battles on the Western Front, in Vietnam, and most recently Iraq, the division has earned a reputation as one of the pre-eminent combat units of the US Army. This book covers the 101st Airborne Division in the Vietnam War, in which it was engaged from 1965 to 1971 as one of two designated airborne divisions (alongside the 1st Air Cavalry).

This was a war unlike any the US Army had been sent to fight before. In places the landscape bore some similarities to certain islands of the Pacific, but it was a very different set of circumstances and a different enemy the soldiers faced. Although superbly equipped and trained, the troops on the ground were hobbled by stringent rules of engagement, often indifferent leadership and the difficulties in fighting an experienced enemy on their own ground. The first US Army advisors sent to Vietnam were soon apprised of the difficulties of transporting men and equipment in Vietnam, with its poorly developed infrastructure and vast swathes of jungle. This in turn prompted the army to develop the airmobile doctrine that was so important to US operations in the theatre. As a pioneer and leading proponent in the field of airborne tactics, the 101st Airborne ultimately made a major contribution.

AIRBORNE ORIGINS

In the early 1900s the inventors of the parachute envisaged it as a means of escaping from stricken aircraft, and in this role it achieved some success in the First World War. In 1918 the US Army planned to use parachutists to break the deadlock on the Western Front, but the end of hostilities curtailed this. It was left to leading US aviation pioneer General 'Billy' Mitchell to take up the banner of dedicated parachute forces, specially trained and equipped to be dropped by aircraft into combat. At a demonstration of his concept at Kelly Field at San Antonio, Texas, six soldiers parachuted from a Martin Bomber, landed safely, and less than three minutes after exiting the aircraft had their weapons assembled and were ready for action. However, US observers quickly dismissed Mitchell's revolutionary idea (and later, his theories on strategic bombing) and the US Army was robbed of an opportunity to take an early lead in the development of airborne forces.

Some of those present on that day were less hasty to arrive at the same conclusion. Among others, senior Soviet and German representatives were favourably impressed with the demonstration, and in succeeding years in the USSR, static line parachuting was introduced as a national sport and the population encouraged to join the fledgling Russian Airborne Corps. In 1927 the Red Army carried out the first experiments with airborne troops and in August 1930, at Voronezh, Russia, its paratroops participated for the first time in the annual military manoeuvres. Their actions proved so effective that a

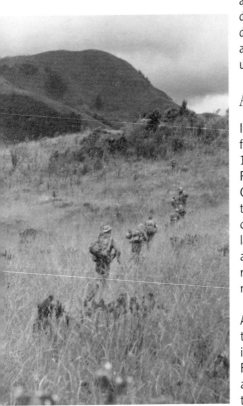

Below: Elements of Company A, 2nd Battalion, 502nd Infantry (Airborne), 1st Brigade, 101st Airborne Division (Separate) move out on patrol from a helicopter landing zone during Operation 'Cook' on 8 September 1967. The beautiful but hostile terrain of Vietnam is well illustrated in this photograph.

repeat performance was given in Moscow a month later. However, the programme lapsed following the execution of its leading proponent, Tukhachevsky, in 1937, and although at the start of the Second World War there were some 100,000 paratroops in the Red Army, these were hardly used at all in their dedicated role.

The German observers also eagerly grasped the idea and planners worked quickly to develop an effective military parachute organisation, leading to the establishment in 1935 of an experimental airborne staff under Kurt Student. Airborne forces were also quickly integrated into the blitzkrieg strategy that was being formalised by German military planners in the interwar years. Under the rapid expansion of the armed forces that accompanied the Nazis' consolidation of power, considerable resources were earmarked for these formations. At the start of the Second World War, Germany's parachute branch undoubtedly led the field, and in the early 'lightning' campaigns in the West her airborne troops spearheaded the assaults on key positions in the enemy rear. One of their most notable feats was the attack on the fortress of Eben Emael on the Albert Canal in Belgium. Here, two of the key assets of the paratrooper – speed and surprise – played a major role in the Belgian defeat.

UNITED STATES

In the United States things got off to a rather slower start. Despite his demonstrations, few of America's military men shared Mitchell's enthusiasm for the potential of aircraft and airborne forces, and little attention was paid to their development. However, the successful employment of airborne troops by the Germans in their invasion of the Low Countries exposed such short-sightedness and provided the much needed spur. US military branches began an all-out effort to develop this new form of warfare, but considerable opposition remained.

In April 1940 the Department of War approved plans for the formation of a test platoon of Airborne Infantry to form, equip, and train under the direction and control of the Army's Infantry Board. In June, the Commandant of the Infantry School was directed to organise a test platoon of volunteers from Fort Benning's 29th Infantry Regiment. Later that year, the 2nd Infantry Division was directed to conduct the necessary tests to develop reference data and operational procedures for air-transported troops.

In July 1940, the task of organising the platoon began. First Lieutenant William T. Ryder of the 29th Infantry Regiment volunteered and was designated the test platoon's Platoon Leader, with Lieutenant James A. Bassett as Assistant Platoon Leader. On the criteria of high standards of health and rugged physical characteristics, 48 enlisted men were selected from a pool of 200 volunteers. Quickly thereafter, the platoon moved into tents near Lawson Field, and an abandoned hangar was obtained for use as a training hall and for parachute packing.

Lieutenant Colonel William C. Lee, a staff officer for the Chief of Infantry, arranged for the men to be moved to the Safe Parachute Company at Hightstown, New Jersey, for training on the parachute drop towers used during the New York World's Fair. Eighteen days after organisation, the platoon was moved to New Jersey and trained for one week on the 250-foot towers.

The army was so impressed with the tower drops that two were purchased and erected at Fort Benning, on what is now Eubanks Field. Later, two more were added. Three of the original four towers are still in use training paratroopers at the base.

Less than 45 days after organisation, the first jump from an aircraft in flight by members of the test platoon was made from a Douglas B-18 over Lawson Field on 16 August 1940. Thirteen days later, also at Lawson Field, the platoon made the first mass jump held in the United States.

Above: Troopers of the 1st Battalion, 327th Infantry (Airborne), 1st Brigade, 101st Airborne Division (Separate) return fire from old Viet Cong trenches as the enemy mounts an attack during Operation 'Hawthorne' on 7 June 1966. Following on from Operation 'Paul Revere', the 1st Brigade accounted for 531 enemy casualties during Operation 'Hawthorne' through massive firepower including 27,000 artillery rounds and 473 US Air Force close air support sorties. US losses were high with 48 dead and 239 wounded but the 1st Brigade was awarded the Presidential Unit Citation (see box on pages 28–9) for what the brigade commander, Brig Gen Willard Pearson, declaimed was 'our biggest and best fight, our greatest battle.'

The first parachute combat unit to be organised was the 501st Parachute Battalion. It was commanded by Major William M. Miley, later a major general and commander of the 17th Airborne Division, and the original test platoon members formed the battalion cadre. The Civilian Conservation Corps cleared new jump areas and three new training buildings were erected. Several B-18 and C-39 aircraft were provided for training.

The 502nd Parachute Infantry Battalion, commanded by Lieutenant Colonel William C. Lee with men from the 501st as a cadre, was activated on 1 July 1941. However, the 502nd was far below its approved strength, and Lieutenant Colonel Lee petitioned the 9th Infantry Division at Fort Bragg, North Carolina, for 172 volunteers. The response was very favourable: more than 400 men volunteered, including many non-commissioned officers who were willing to take a reduction in rank to transfer to the new battalion.

In December 1941 the path of history took another turn, when Japan attacked the US Naval Base at Pearl Harbour. The British Army had by this time successfully used parachute infantry in combat, prompting the US Army to authorise the raising of two Airborne Infantry Divisions: 82nd and 101st Airborne. On 15 August, the 101st Airborne Division (Air Assault) was activated at Camp Claiborne, Louisiana. The 101st Division had originally been activated on 23 July 1918 as part of the mobilisation for the First World War. However, because weapons, ammunition and other supplies were scarce for training, it was never fully organised or manned. After the war was over, the unit was demobilised, but it was reconstituted as the 101st Infantry Division in 1921, as part of a build-up of reserves, and made its headquarters in Milwaukee, Wisconsin. For the most part it was a paper division with little in the way of real units, and it remained that way until the United States entered the Second World War.

At the activation ceremony on 19 August 1942, the first commander, Major General William C. Lee, issued the following now-famous order to his new recruits. It reads:

'The 101st Airborne Division, activated at Camp Claiborne, Louisiana, has no history, but it has a rendezvous with destiny. Like the early American pioneers whose invincible courage was the foundation stone of this nation, we have broken with the past and its traditions in order to establish our claim to the future.

'Due to the nature of our armament, and the tactics in which we shall perfect ourselves, we shall be called upon to carry out operations of far-reaching military importance and we shall habitually go into action when the need is immediate and extreme.

'Let me call your attention to the fact that our badge is the great American eagle. This is a fitting emblem for a division that will crush its enemies by falling upon them like a thunderbolt from the skies.

'The history we shall make, the record of high achievement we hope to write in the annals of the American Army and the American people, depends wholly and completely on the men of this division. Each individual, each officer and each enlisted man, must therefore regard himself as a necessary part of a complex and powerful instrument for the overcoming of the enemies of the nation. Each, in his own job, must realise that he is not only a means, but an indispensable means for obtaining the goal of victory. It is, therefore, not too much to say that the future itself, in whose molding we expect to have our share, is in the hands of the soldiers of the 101st Airborne Division.'

TRAINING

With the expansion of the airborne force, it became apparent that a centralised training facility should be established. Consequently, a facility was organised at Fort Benning, Georgia, on 15 May 1942. In October, the 101st Airborne reported there to begin parachute and combat training. The programme was intense, and unforgiving. As well as being required to master basic infantry skills, the troops had to learn entirely new ways of fighting a war. A significant number of the men entering the programme 'washed out' in the first few days. According to statistics given in Stephen Ambrose's book, *Band of Brothers*, only 148 out of 500 officer volunteers were accepted into the airborne forces; only 1,800 graduated from the training out of every 5,300 enlisted men.

At first the parachute troops and the glider troops trained separately, but from early 1943 as a division. With this training completed by June, 506th Parachute Infantry Regiment was added to the ranks of the 101st Airborne just in time for the Second Army manoeuvres, in which the division was given the opportunity to prove itself fully prepared for battle. In July 1943, the unit was certified as combat ready and began to move to embarkation points in New York, from where on 5 September, it set sail for England.

PREPARING FOR WAR

The passage across the grey, U-boat infested waters of the North Atlantic, though cramped and tedious, passed without incident. Safely conveyed to England, the 101st was quartered in Wiltshire and Berkshire to wait until all the personnel and equipment could be transported across the Atlantic. The division then commenced advanced training in night fighting, urban warfare, German equipment familiarisation, land navigation and many other skills. In addition, a jump school was established to certify the new units then being added to the divisional roster.

The early months of 1944 were a time of change. In January the 101st received its third parachute regiment, the 501st Parachute Infantry. On 5 February General Lee, who had championed the airborne cause from the beginning, suffered a heart attack. Although he had brought the division from its initial organisation through training for the fight in Europe, General Lee was not to be part of the 101st's baptism of fire. He was relieved of his command and returned to the United States. Brigadier General Maxwell D. Taylor, former commander of the 82nd Airborne Division Artillery who went on to become one of America's most famous generals, assumed command on 14 March.

The division underwent another organisational change that month, when 2nd Battalion, 401st Glider Infantry, was permanently transferred to the 82nd Airborne Division. The 1st Battalion was attached to the 327th Glider Infantry to operate under that regiment as a third battalion. (1st Battalion, 401st Glider Infantry Regiment, was made an official element of 327th Glider Infantry Regiment in April 1945.)

In March, a demonstration of American military prowess was staged for the British Prime Minister Winston Churchill, Supreme Allied Commander General Dwight D. Eisenhower, and dozens of high ranking civilian and military officials. The 101st was tasked with demonstrating airborne operations, and so successful was this, and Division Artillery Commander McAuliffe's briefing to Churchill and Eisenhower on the capabilities of the 101st Airborne Division, that it was chosen to spearhead the assault on Europe.

Shortly after this demonstration, Taylor received his orders for Operation 'Overlord'. Training intensified and culminated with three large-scale operations – 'Beaver', 'Tiger' and 'Eagle' – that were designed to familiarise the soldiers with conditions they would encounter in France.

During Operation 'Beaver', at Slapton Sands on the Devonshire coast, elements of the division jumped from trucks instead of planes with the mission of capturing the causeway bridges that crossed the estuary behind the beach. The division performed much the same mission during the second exercise, Operation 'Tiger'.

Operation 'Eagle', held during the second week of May, was the division's dress rehearsal for its role in the coming Normandy invasion. The 101st, this time jumping from actual planes, was once again assigned to capture the causeways leading away from a

Above: The pathfinder unit of the 101st Airborne Division, dropped by parachute, sets up radar equipment near Bastogne, Belgium, 23 December 1944. It is their job to guide planes with medical supplies and ammunition to the division, besieged by the Germans during the Battle of the Bulge.

H&HC, 101st Airborne Division cited in War Department General Orders 4, 12 January 1945:

The 101st Airborne Division Headquarters and Headquarters Company is cited for extraordinary heroism and outstanding performance of duty in action in the initial assault on the northern coast of Normandy, France. Before daylight on the morning of 6 June 1944, the parachute and glider echelon of this unit landed in the vicinity of St Come-du-Mont, France. They were widely dispersed initially because of a bad drop and encountered heavy enemy fire delivered from strongly fortified positions. Many fierce and vicious battles took place between small detachments of airborne soldiers and strongly emplaced enemy forces as the parachutists and glider men moved to assemble and to their objectives. Innumerable acts of gallantry and self-sacrifice were performed in the determined and successful efforts of the officers and men of the 101st Airborne Division Headquarters and Headquarters Company. Although this unit was chiefly composed of clerks, technicians, and specialists, usually not considered as combat soldiers, they wiped out many enemy pill boxes, artillery positions, and other fortifications. Under extremely difficult conditions they established the division command post at the predesignated location, established contact with the scattered elements of the division and organised them into a unified command which successfully accomplished its mission of insuring the establishment of the beachhead Utah. The second glider echelon landed near Hiesville, France, on the evening of D-Day. Despite heavy enemy resistance encountered at the landing fields, this group successfully reached the division command post and augmented the command group then operating the command post. The combined efforts of

simulated beach. Although a misunderstanding caused most of the division to jump at the wrong coordinates, the mission was accomplished and the exercise was considered a success. The division then returned to its stations to continue preparation for the coming battles on the continent.

INTO EUROPE

In late May, with D-Day imminent, the 101st left their training areas and moved to their staging and jump-off points. The division had been given the mission of landing behind enemy lines in the area designated as Utah beach on the Cherbourg Peninsula. Once on the ground they were to clear the exit points from Utah for the 4th Infantry Division's breakout. In addition they were to prevent any reinforcements from reaching Utah.

On the night of 5–6 June, the pathfinders of the 101st became the first Americans to set foot in occupied France. After they had cleared the way for the 1st and 4th Infantry Divisions behind Utah Beach, a bitter battle developed for the town of Carentan. This and subsequent battles for the bridgehead raged over the following month; the 101st Airborne was fighting almost continuously, until it returned to England in July to prepare for the liberation of Holland – Operation 'Market Garden'.

Under this operation, on 17 September 1944, the division seized and held the Eindhoven–Arnhem corridor for 10 days against heavy odds and spent a total of 72 days in battle. In November the 101st returned to France to rest and re-equip, only to be called to action again in December as Hitler unleashed his offensive through the Ardennes. While guarding the crucial transportation hub of Bastogne, Belgium, the division was surrounded by advancing enemy forces. Called on to surrender by his German adversary, divisional commander Brigadier General Anthony McAuliffe gave the brusque retort 'Nuts!' and the unit fought on until the 8-day-long siege was lifted.

Following the siege of Bastogne, the 101st was ordered into the Ruhr area of Germany, but without 501st Parachute Regiment, which was ordered into reserve and began training for a possible rescue attempt of Allied prisoners of war. However, due to a shortage of transport aircraft and the relatively low priority of the mission, this operation was never mounted.

The other elements of the 101st took part in operations to reduce one of the few remaining cohesive German Army Groups, which was concentrated in the Ruhr River region of Germany. In the beginning of April, the US First and Ninth Armies attacked and by the end of the month, the German forces within the pocket had largely been eliminated; 325,000 prisoners fell into Allied hands.

The final mission for the 101st was an assault on Hitler's retreat at Berchtesgaden in conjunction with 3rd Infantry Division. Here the division accepted the surrender of the German XIII SS and LXXXII Corps, and also took prisoner several key members of the Nazi regime who were later brought before the War Crimes Tribunal at the Hague – Field Marshal Albert Kesselring, Julius Streicher, the anti-Semitic editor of *Der Sturmer*, and Obergruppenführer Karl Oberg, the chief of German SS in occupied France. Colonel General Heinz Guderian, the armour expert, was another of their prisoners.

The 101st remained in Germany on occupation duty until November 1945, when it was deactivated in France and shipped home. During the Second World War, the division spent 214 days in combat. For their deeds during the conflict, the 'The Battered Bastards of Bastogne' were awarded four campaign streamers and two Presidential Unit Citations, in addition to two Medals of Honor. Soldiers of the 101st Airborne Division were awarded 47 Distinguished Service Crosses, 516 Silver Stars and 6,977 Bronze Stars.

POSTWAR

The 101st Airborne was reactivated as a training unit at Camp Breckinridge, Kentucky, in 1948 and again in 1950. Although it did not fight in the Korean War, it was responsible for training the 11th Airborne Division, which served with honour.

It was reactivated once again in 1954 at Fort Jackson, South Carolina, and in March 1956 the 101st was transferred, less personnel and equipment, to Fort Campbell, Kentucky, to be reorganised as a combat division. The division colours were unsheathed and presented there on 21 September 1956, and since that time Fort Campbell has been its home base. In the years to follow, the 101st continued to train paratroopers. Then in 1965 it was informed that it was being shipped to Vietnam to fight the war that was escalating in that country. In the words of Major General B.E. Powell, US Army Division Commander in 1965:

'The history of the 101st Airborne Division was not to end, finally, with the triumph of American arms on the battlefields of WWII. To meet the rising challenge of Communist imperialism, its colors were uncased and the best of a new generation of soldiers was chosen to fill its ranks again. Today, ever ready to keep its "Rendezvous With Destiny," the Division of that new generation does credit to the great heritage of Bastogne. The place of the 101st is secure in the annals of history; its exploits in combat will be remembered for as long as men honor the memory of valor.'

A brief history of the origins of each brigade follows.

1st Brigade

The major organic unit in the 1st Brigade was the 327th Infantry Regiment, composed of the 'Above the Rest', 'No Slack' and 'Battle Force' Battalions. The regiment traces its history to the 164th Infantry Brigade of the 82nd Infantry Division formed on 17 September 1917 at Fort Gordon, Georgia. That unit, too, has a long history of campaigns and honours. The 'Bastogne' Brigade has been involved in three conflicts and one peacekeeping mission: As well as fighting in the First World War, during the Second World War, it participated in the Normandy, Ardennes–Alsace, Rhineland, and Central European campaigns.

2nd Brigade

Headquarters and Headquarters Company, 2nd Brigade, traces its lineage to the 159th Infantry Brigade, an element of the 80th Division, organised in August 1917. During the First World War, the 159th Infantry Brigade participated in the Picardy (1918), Somme (1918), and Meuse–Argonne campaigns against the Imperial German Army.

Reorganised as the 80th Reconnaissance Troop (Mechanized) of the 80th Infantry Division, the unit participated in the Northern France, Rhineland, Ardennes–Alsace and Central European campaigns against Germany in the Second World War.

A major reorganisation took place on 3 February 1964, when the 2nd Brigade of the 101st Airborne Division was activated at Fort Campbell, replacing the 1st Airborne Battle Group 501st Infantry Regiment. The new 2nd Brigade's original organic battalions were the 1st and 2nd Battalions, 501st Infantry, and the 1st Battalion, 502nd Infantry.

3rd Brigade

The 3rd Brigade, 101st Airborne Division (Air Assault), traces its lineage back to the organisation of Headquarters, 160th Infantry Brigade. This was organised in August 1917 as an element of the 80th Division at Camp Lee, Virginia. Through numerous

---

the 101st Airborne Division Headquarters and Headquarters Company in establishing and protecting the division command post in the face of bitter enemy resistance permitted the Commanding General and his staff to formulate and direct the successful execution of the plans for the division.

Presidential Unit Citation (Army), Streamer embroidered BASTOGNE

101st Airborne Division (less 2d Battalion, 401st Glider Infantry Regiment) cited in War Department General Orders 17, 13 March 1945 (along with other attached units):

These units distinguished themselves in combat against powerful and aggressive enemy forces composed of elements of eight German divisions during the period from 18 to 27 December 1944 by extraordinary heroism and gallantry in defense of the key communications center of Bastogne, Belgium. Essential to a large-scale exploitation of his break-through into Belgium and northern Luxembourg, the enemy attempted to seize Bastogne by attacking constantly and savagely with the best of his armor and infantry. Without benefit of prepared defenses, facing almost overwhelming odds and with very limited and fast-dwindling supplies, these units maintained a high combat morale and an impenetrable defense despite extremely heavy bombing, intense artillery fire, and constant attacks from infantry and armor on all sides of their completely cut-off and encircled position. This masterful and grimly determined defense denied the enemy even momentary success in an operation for which he paid dearly in men materiel and eventually morale. The outstanding courage, resourcefulness, and undaunted determination of this gallant force are in keeping with the highest traditions of the service.

reorganisations and redesignations, Headquarters and Headquarters Company, 3rd Brigade, evolved into its modern configuration in February 1964. In Vietnam, the Brigade comprised three infantry battalions, 3rd Battalion, 187th Infantry Regiment, and the 1st and 2nd Battalions of the 506th Infantry Regiment. Between 1964 and 1967 these units conducted operations in various locations ranging from the Mojave Desert to Norway, where it prepared for both conventional and unconventional war contingencies.

101st Aviation Brigade

On 1 July 1968, at Camp Eagle in the Republic of Vietnam, the 160th Aviation Group was constituted. On 25 June 1969, the 160th was redesignated as the 101st Aviation Group. With the air mobility concept added to the organic capabilities of the 101st Airborne Division, 101st Aviation Group was attached to it. The 101st Aviation Group served from the Delta to the DMZ, and from the east coast to Cambodia and Laos, and in 1972 returned to Fort Campbell, Kentucky with the other units of the 101st.

159th Aviation Battalion

The 159th Aviation was originally formed as the 159th Aviation Battalion in Vietnam on 1 July 1968, from the dissolved 308th Combat Aviation Battalion. Organised as the medium and heavy lift Assault Support Helicopter Battalion (ASHB) of the 101st Airborne Division, the unit was composed of three CH-47 companies and one CH-54 company. In February 1972, the 159th ASHB returned to Fort Campbell.

In July of 1965, the first element of the 101st Airborne Division was deployed to the Republic of South Vietnam. The remainder of the division arrived in South Vietnam in October and November of 1967.

In 1965, the 101st Airborne consisted of three brigades, each consisting of three battalions. The 1st 'Bastogne' Brigade deployed to Vietnam in 1965, and was joined in 1967 by the other two.

Below: Brigadier General Anthony C. McAuliffe, artillery commander of the 101st Airborne Division, gives his men last-minute instructions before the take-off from England during Operation 'Market Garden', September 1944.

READY FOR WAR

RECRUITMENT AND TRAINING

The level of professionalism that distinguished the rank and file troops of the 101st Airborne Division from their peers can largely be attributed to thorough and exacting training and to the way in which they were recruited.

Although the division drew from the same pool of manpower as other units, recruitment into the airborne/airmobile units of the US Army has always been on a volunteer basis. No man was or is ever drafted in 'off the street' so to speak. However, there were many conscripts who, having been drafted into the military, volunteered for service in the airborne.

Men came from all backgrounds and walks of life and from every corner of the Union, ensuring that there was no regional bias in the unit. Typically, recruits enlisted, or were drafted into the US Army, after a year or two of college, or else straight from school, at the age of 18–20.

Those wishing to join the Airborne Infantry first had to pass the induction exams that qualified them to begin basic training. After completing Basic Training recruits embarked on Advanced Infantry Training. With these two stages successfully completed they moved on to Airborne School at Fort Benning, Georgia.

Army basic training, a rite of passage for generations of soldiers, is designed to transform civilians into fighters by teaching them to march, shoot rifles and kill the enemy. However, a fundamental problem existed in the mid-1960s in the fact that most of the US armed forces training programme was based on the likelihood of a war on the central European plain against regular forces. Their equipment in many ways reflected this, with much of it was badly suited to conditions in Vietnam. The US Army thus made changes to the programme to accommodate the peculiarities of the war in Southeast Asia. Starting in the 1960s, recruits were also taught how to detect and avoid booby traps, how to search suspected Viet Cong bolt holes, and personal health and hygiene guidelines for tropical climes.

Every 101st Airborne recruit attended basic training in these skills for a minimum of eight weeks, at any one of a number of designated training centres, including among others Fort Bliss, Texas, and Fort Ord, California. During basic training, the recruit was taught how to march in close order, clean, press, shine, salute and all the rest of those military staples. There was also instruction in how to fight using rifle, bayonet, hand grenade and hand to hand combat techniques, and procedures for dealing with tear gas. Those old enough might also receive training in how to drive military trucks and jeeps.

The recruits were tested and graded in each of these skills, and those who qualified with high marks might be rewarded with a weekend pass. Those who attained sufficiently high marks in the military entry exams might have qualified to go to Officer Candidate School.

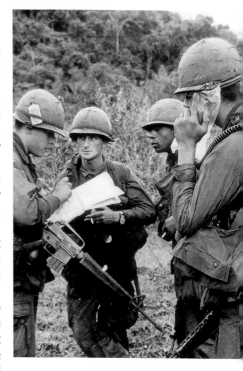

Above: There is an old military adage – 'There is nothing more dangerous than a young officer with a map'. With the high turnover of officers who did six-month tours of duty in the field to 12 months for the other ranks, the knowledge and experience of the NCOs were vital for unit cohesion and success or survival in the field. Here, with their RTOs close to hand, the company commander and platoon leaders of Company C, 2nd Battalion, 327th Infantry (Airborne), 1st Brigade, 101st Airborne Division (Separate), confer during Operation 'Geronimo I' near Tuy Hoa on 22 November 1966.

After basic training recruits were promoted to Private E-2 and sent to advanced infantry training (AIT) school, typically at Fort Dix in New Jersey, or Fort Gordon, Georgia, where they learned more about how to survive on the battlefield. There was more training with the M-14 rifle or the new M-16 rifle (depending on the period), M-60 machine gun and other infantry weapons. Recruits learnt small unit tactics, and how to fire and move as teams in combat. There was further practice in musketry on the ranges, and a much feared Survival, Evasion and Escape course. Those trainees who were captured while trying to evade their pursuers on this course were usually left with a lasting mental and physical impression of the experience.

On graduation from AIT, airborne hopefuls were promoted to Private First Class (Pfc. E-3), and sent to the Basic Airborne Course (BAC) at Fort Benning, Georgia, home of the US Army Airborne School. However, after the 101st Airborne became an airmobile unit, troopers were no longer required to qualify as parachutists. Prospective officers reported to Officer Candidate School, also located at Fort Benning.

In Vietnam the 101st Airborne established its own Replacement Training School at Camp Ray.

AIRBORNE TRAINING

Things began to get a lot tougher when the recruit embarked on the BAC. The first aim of this course was to qualify the recruit in the use of the parachute as a means of combat deployment, by building up his confidence to jump from an aircraft while in flight.

The second goal was to develop leadership, self-confidence and an aggressive spirit through mental and physical conditioning.

The third was to maintain the level of physical fitness required of a military parachutist through daily physical training. It was, however, assumed that any recruit who started the physically gruelling course at Fort Benning had thus far attained a high level of personal physical fitness. The physically weak were more likely either not to complete the course because of an injury, or to fail due to an inability to qualify on the training apparatuses. PT sessions were on the menu for the first and last period each day, and in between there were seven hours of demanding, vigorous training. The physical training programme placed great emphasis on squad runs, in either gym gear or Full Battle Order, with as many as five of these in one day. Failure to complete two of these in any one week resulted in disqualification from the course.

Running concurrently with this PT programme, the airborne instruction undertaken at Fort Benning was divided into three phases: a ground training phase, tower training phase and jump training phase.

During the ground phase, recruits were subject to an intensive programme of instruction to build individual airborne skills, and prepare them to make a parachute jump and land safely. This included training on a mock aircraft door, a 34-foot tower, and an apparatus that replicated the sensation of lateral drift (LDA). To go forward to tower training week, they had to qualify on the 34-foot tower and the LDA, and pass all PT requirements.

The individual skills learned during the ground phase were refined during a week during which the recruits trained on the 34-foot towers, swing landing trainer (SLT), a mock aircraft door for mass-exit training, and suspended harness. All these were intended to build individual and team skills. To go forward to jump training week, recruits had to qualify on the SLT, master the mass-exit procedures from the 34-foot tower, and pass all PT requirements. Following on from this, there was another week of training, this time using real aircraft, at the end of which the coveted 'wings' were awarded at a special graduation ceremony.

Above: Personnel of the 1st Brigade, 101st Airborne Division (Separate), jump from a CV2 Caribou during a demonstration at Dong Ba Thien on 29 July 1965 to mark the arrival of the 3,700 men of the 1st Brigade at Cam Ranh Bay where they disembarked from the World War II Liberty ship, USNS *General Leroy Eltinge* after a three-week ocean voyage. They were met by two former commanders of the 101st Airborne Division, Maxwell D. Taylor, US Ambassador to South Vietnam, and General William W. Westmoreland, commander of MACV.

It should be noted however that from the late 1960s, as the 101st moved from an Airborne to an Airmobile Division, the Airborne School switched its focus away from parachute operations and was used to teach rappelling skills.

After completing the BAC, or rappelling instruction, recruits moved to Fort Campbell, Kentucky, to embark on a course of jungle training.

The US Army Jumpmaster School, also at Fort Benning, trained select personnel in the skills necessary to lead a combat-equipped jump. The Pathfinder School course taught procedures for establishing and operating day/night helicopter landing zones and parachute drop zones, slingload operations, and air traffic control.

DEPLOYMENT OF 1ST BRIGADE

In the wake of the Gulf of Tonkin incident, US intervention in Vietnam was escalated dramatically. Late in the winter of 1965 President Lyndon B. Johnson announced that US forces in Vietnam would be raised from 75,000 to 125,000 and that additional forces would be sent as requested.

The Marines were first to deploy, around Da Nang, followed by 173rd Airborne Brigade. In the spring the 101st Airborne Division was alerted that it was to send a brigade of infantry plus support troops to Vietnam in the summer. Clearly, this gave the division staff little time to carry out the myriad of necessary preparations. Furthermore, it was unclear for how long the unit was expected to deploy, adding to the administrative headaches.

Prior to the movement by sea of the main body, an advance party flew to Nha Trang in two ageing C-124 aircraft; because of mechanical and administrative difficulties, the journey took a week. The main body of over 3,600 troops was flown from Fort Campbell on the evening of 6 July to San Francisco, where they took buses to Oakland Army Terminal. Here they were greeted by an Army band, Red Cross 'Donut Dollies', and saw for the first time the grey ship that was to ferry them to war on the other side of the world.

The USNS *General Leroy Eltinge* was 510 feet long, every inch painted grey. The ship departed Alameda Navy Yard on 9 July. It was not a happy passage. Into the *Eltinge,* which had a normal capacity of 2,200, were crammed 3,600 men, the bulk of the brigade's manpower. Furthermore, during the voyage there were problems with the electricity, plumbing and a lack of ventilation below decks, which added to the men's misery at being cooped up. The *Eltinge* also broke down while crossing the Pacific, bobbing around without power for about a day and then limping into Subic Bay for repairs.

Finally, on 29 July, the ship arrived at Cam Ranh Bay, where two former, distinguished commanders of the 101st Airborne Division, Maxwell D. Taylor, Ambassador to South Vietnam, and General William C. Westmoreland, commander of MACV, were there to officially welcome the men of the 1st Brigade to Vietnam.

Until 21 August, the brigade manned a defensive perimeter in the Cam Ranh Bay area. During this initial deployment and on subsequent operations, the troops familiarised themselves with new equipment and brigade structure, and conducted exercises in airmobile operations. However, they found that many of the items that they had brought into the country, such as camouflage nets, were completely extraneous and many things they had not brought, such as additional water trucks, were absolutely essential.

Three weeks after arriving in Vietnam the brigade moved to Binh Dinh Province in II Corps to commence combat operations under Operation 'Highland'.

Above: Pfc. Rodger Lyle of the 1st Brigade, 101st Airborne Division (Separate), wields a chainsaw as he clears trees and scrub to create a landing zone for resupply helicopters during Operation 'Austin VI', a search and destroy mission against the VC/NVA operating in Phuoc Long and Quang Duc Provinces near the Cambodian border on 15 May 1966. Operation 'Austin VI' was conducted to block NVA infiltration routes from Cambodia.

DEPLOYMENT OF 2ND AND 3RD BRIGADES

Nearly two years after the 1st Brigade was sent to Southeast Asia, in the late spring of 1967 the 2nd and 3rd Brigades were ordered to make ready for a move to Vietnam, scheduled for February of the next year.

Preparations began immediately. Between 22 May and 3 June, the two brigades conducted a war game, Operation 'Goblin Hunt I', in Stewart County, Tennessee. The 3rd Battalion of the 506th Infantry teamed with Special Forces teams to provide the aggressor force for this exercise, which was designed to familiarise the men with the kind of tactics employed by the Viet Cong (VC). Then in mid-July Operation 'Crocigator' was staged in the swamps surrounding Fort Stewart, Georgia, to demonstrate to the men the problems of fighting in such an environment.

In the last week of the month there was a slight interruption to the training schedule when the 101st Airborne Division received an Executive Order from President Johnson to help restore order in Detroit, where serious race riots had broken out. After training in riot control techniques some 4,700 paratroopers were airlifted to the city, where they helped to restore order.

In August, after the units returned to Fort Campbell, operation-readiness tests were conducted. There was also a spell of mountain training in the Cherokee National Forest in Tennessee, to train the men and leaders in small unit tactics in mountainous terrain.

Preparation for overseas movement began on 24 August. This was a huge administrative task, requiring every individual's health, dental and ID records to be checked. There was more training and unit photographs, and training on Viet Cong mines, booby traps, and mine warfare techniques at Viet Cong village at Fort Campbell. Battalion Officers and NCOs attended Combat Intelligence Training,

On 2 October the 3rd Battalion of the 506th Infantry departed from Fort Campbell, travelled via commercial airlines to San Francisco, California, and boarded the USNS *General William Weigel* at Oakland Naval Base. Next day, the ship steamed out of San Francisco for South Vietnam. After a 19-day passage, it docked on the west coast of Vietnam at Qui Nhon to let off the 3rd Battalion; the 173rd Airborne Brigade, disembarked at Vung Tau the following day and finally arrived at Cam Ranh Bay on 26 October. After barely two weeks of training the battalion was thrust into its first combat assault on 11 November 1967.

The remaining units of 2nd and 3rd Brigades were airlifted to Vietnam in December during Operation 'Eagle Lift', which is detailed in the next chapter.

TACTICS

From the perspective of most ground commanders, the primary purpose of tactical ground operations in Vietnam was to defeat enemy forces. Consequently, 'find, fix, fight, and finish' the enemy became a much-repeated slogan during the Vietnam War.

In jungle operations, small-unit tactics were essential, since heavy vegetation and broken terrain provided ideal concealment for the enemy. One former battalion commander stated: 'As I saw the war in Vietnam, it belonged to the company commander. He was the key to success – a planner, a doer, an independent operator, and a leader of men.'

The key aspect of the Vietnam War was the very widespread use of helicopters by the US and its allies, which emerged as one of the most important innovations of the conflict. From the initial phases of US participation, the helicopter's great mobility and carrying capacity provided the essential ingredient for operations against the enemy's light infantry in the diverse terrain of Southeast Asia. As a means of transporting supplies,

Below: UH-1D helicopters loaded with personnel of 2nd Battalion, 502nd Infantry, fly over a small Vietnamese village on way to combat area during Operation 'Harrison' near Tuy Hoa.

ammunition, equipment and wounded personnel, its functions ranged far beyond being simply a combat vehicle. Only the helicopter could accomplish such a variety of tactical tasks, ranging from the insertion of a long-range patrol to the vertical assault of an entire division.

Employment of the helicopter enabled allied forces to mass men and equipment in a fashion that affected tactical methods fundamentally. They could transport units to a battle area and could enable them to manoeuvre or to reinforce, displace or withdraw combat power during the battle. They could also be used to concentrate forces quickly. The dominant characteristic of the development of infantry organisations and tactics during the war was the increasing application of airmobile concepts and tactics.

Armed helicopter and aerial rocket artillery (ARA) also provided important support to ground units. Helicopters armed with machine guns, rockets and grenade launchers provided light fire support, which was particularly effective against enemy troops in the open or without fortifications. ARA units provided heavier fire support, often in areas beyond the range of a unit's direct support artillery. Highly mobile, the ARA units could answer calls for fire over extremely large areas, and along with armed helicopters provided especially important support in air assault operations.

OPERATIONS

Search-and-destroy operations

Three basic types of operations were conducted in Vietnam. The first type aimed to 'search and destroy'. Operations of this type sought to locate the enemy and destroy him, and variations could be conducted from company to multidivisional level, though the norm was a multi-battalion operation. In April 1968, the Army dropped the term 'search and destroy' since it was, as General Westmoreland noted, 'equated in the (American) public mind with aimless searches in the jungle and destruction of property'. Other terms, such as combat sweep, reconnaissance in force and spoiling attack, replaced the phrase 'search and destroy'.

Clearing operations

Although 'clearing' operations resembled search-and-destroy operations, they usually placed a greater emphasis on pacification. While search-and-destroy operations chased enemy forces from an area or destroyed them, clearing operations kept them off balance and allowed the South Vietnamese government to extend its influence into the area.

Reconnaissances in force, combat sweeps or other offensive operations continued to be conducted, but the greatest emphasis in clearing operations was placed on eliminating local or main force enemy resistance and destroying his support base. Local commanders and political authorities, for example, often used cordon-and-search operations to 'clear' a village or area. Thus, clearing operations usually lasted longer than search-and-destroy operations.

Securing operations

The final activity was the 'securing' operation. These operations protected pacification accomplishments, but concentrated on eliminating local guerrilla units and the enemy's political infrastructure and support base. Although multi-battalion offensive sweeps could be used to secure an area, the norm was probably saturation patrolling and cordon and searches of hamlets.

Theoretically, the proper sequence of operations was, first, search and destroy, and second, clear and secure, with the final phase being dominated by the South Vietnamese Regional and Popular Forces and the police. While search-and-destroy operations

AIRMOBILITY

Airmobility was a tactical doctrine that began to be developed by the US Army in the early 1960s, entailing the use of helicopters to find the enemy, carry troops into battle, provide them with gunship support, position artillery, and provide communications and resupply. In Vietnam, although the Allied ground forces made extensive use of helicopters, 1st Cavalry and 101st Airborne were the only divisions with their own dedicated aircraft, and during that time, these pioneering airborne units helped further the development of airmobile concepts.

Studies on the viability of airmobility were initiated by the Army Concept Team in 1962 for Army of the Republic of Vietnam (ARVN) and entailed the uplift into combat of fighting troops by H-21 Shawnee helicopters. The trials proved successful and led to the raising of the first dedicated airmobile division, 1st Cavalry. In 1968, 101st Airborne became the second such unit when it was redesignated as 101st Airborne Division (Airmobile). Between 1965 and 1971 the 'Screaming Eagles' employed airmobile tactics in seven of the 15 major ground offensives in which they were engaged, out of a total of 17 launched by US forces in the Vietnam War.

engaged the enemy's main force and provincial battalions, the remaining smaller elements were rooted out in clearing and securing operations.

The tactics employed by American ground troops in South Vietnam were heavily influenced by the enemy's organisation and tactics. Because of their detailed knowledge of local terrain, extensive combat experience in guerrilla warfare and often intense dedication to their cause, VC soldiers were formidable opponents throughout the war. People's Army of Vietnam (PAVN) units were better equipped than the VC units and usually operated as battalions, regiments or even divisions. Except for their greater firepower and usually larger units, PAVN methods of operation resembled those of main force Vietcong.

The VC and PAVN used essentially infantry tactics, and mobility was the key to all their operations, from the small actions of the local forces to the larger actions of the regular forces. The enemy rarely accepted battle in unfavourable situations and only accepted decisive contact under exceptional circumstances. Their operations were usually ruled by Sun Tzu's maxim, 'When the enemy advances, withdraw; when he defends, harass; when he is tired, attack; when he withdraws, pursue'.

VC and PAVN units used several techniques to weaken the effects of the allied firepower. One of the most important of these was night fighting. Their ability to operate at night under the concealment of darkness often served to nullify the overwhelming firepower advantage of an American unit.

If the Vietcong or North Vietnamese Army were forced to defend or were to remain immobile for a period, as at Dong Ap Bia (see next chapter), they built elaborate networks of trenches, bunkers and tunnels that provided protection against the firepower of attacking allied units. The enemy also engaged allied units at very close distances, especially in jungle fighting, thereby limiting the allied use of artillery, air strikes and helicopter support. Their stress on surprise and mobility also enabled them to strike and escape before allied firepower could be concentrated against them.

Some of the most successful techniques for finding the enemy involved the helicopter. Air assaults struck suspected enemy locations, and a series of successive assaults often checked a number of areas for possible enemy presence. A variation on this emphasised the insertion of small assault forces into a number of potential areas where the enemy might be located. The helicopter also provided an easy method for reconnoitring large areas. Decoy helicopters could be used to draw enemy fire, and 'Eagle Flights' consisting of approximately one heliborne infantry platoon could develop the situation. The helicopter's mobility permitted commanders to extend their influence over areas vastly greater than they could otherwise have done.

After enemy contact was established, mobile US troops reinforced the unit in contact and encircled the enemy's position. These were the first steps in what came to be called 'pile-on' tactics. If there was any manoeuvre, it usually occurred before contact was made or during the 'pile on' of additional troops and equipment.

Using the great mobility of heliborne or mechanized forces, units occupied blocking or ambush positions in order to destroy fleeing enemy forces. According to the size of forces and area involved, such encircling methods were sometimes called 'rat-hole' or 'bull's-eye' tactics.

During and following the concentration of US forces, attacks were usually conducted by fire rather than by ground assault. Under normal circumstances, an infantry assault was avoided or was delayed until after the enemy had been virtually destroyed by supporting fire. The high proportion of automatic weapons among the enemy caused heavy loss rates in assaulting and exposed allied troops. The function of ground forces (especially the infantry) thus became the 'finding' and 'fixing' of the enemy, but the 'fighting' and 'finishing' were most often accomplished by massive artillery and air firepower. Such tactics minimised American casualties and made maximum use of the overwhelming US advantage in firepower. The standing operating procedure for most units became, 'Save lives, not ammunition'.

Thus, the need to provide adequate fire support clearly affected the conduct of ground operations. The establishing of fire support bases often became the first step in major operations. While this sometimes revealed an upcoming operation to the enemy, the deceptive emplacement of fire support bases tended to keep the enemy guessing about allied intentions. The emphasis on operating from and defending these bases, however, led to what General Westmoreland described as a 'fire base psychosis'. American commanders were reluctant to operate beyond the support of their artillery and to risk fighting on near-equal terms with VC or PAVN units. While this excessive caution detracted from the manoeuvre and offensive capabilities of US units, it minimised American casualties.

Left: Troopers of 2nd Battalion, 502nd Infantry (Airborne), 1st Brigade, 101st Airborne Division (Separate), congregate at the pick-up zone for a combat air assault by UH-1D helicopters during Operation 'Harrison' on 27 February 1966. During its service in Vietnam as the 1st Brigade, 101st Airborne Division (Separate) until the arrival of the complete division in November 1967, the troopers of the 'Screaming Eagles' undertook 31 tactical deployments covering more than 2,500 miles together with 25 major operations. Acting as a 'fire brigade' formation across the country, the 1st Brigade, 101st Airborne Division (Separate), dubbed themselves as the 'Nomads of Vietnam'.

Below: The long-range recon team of the 1st Brigade, 101st Airborne, prepares for Operation 'Harrison' near Tuy Hoa, February 1966.

IN ACTION

VIETNAM

For the duration of the war Vietnam was divided into three military zones – I, II and III Corps. Although 101st Airborne conducted military operations in all three Corps, it was primarily engaged in the northern five provinces of South Vietnam, which made up I Corps, and throughout most of the war shared responsibility for this zone with III Marine Amphibious Force and the Americal Division. The Demilitarized Zone formed the northern border and Laos was to its west. The A Shau Valley in western I Corps was a major terminus of the Ho Chi Minh Trail and a logistical staging area for the North Vietnamese. The major cities in this area were Quang Tri, Hue, Da Nang, Tam Ky and Quang Ngai. Unlike the rest of Vietnam, from the outset the war in I Corps was essentially against North Vietnamese regulars, organised as regiments and divisions, and suported by artillery. More than half of all US casualties occurred in I Corps.

Prefacing more specific information on the actions of the 101st Airborne Division, a brief overview of policy and overall strategy for each phase of US involvement in Vietnam is given, in chronological sequence beginning in 1965 and ending in 1971. This it is hoped will give the reader a clearer overall picture of the war.

DEFENCE

8 March–24 December 1965

Beginning in 1964, PAVN and VC forces infiltrating via the Ho Chi Minh Trail attempted to cut South Vietnam in two from the Central Highlands to the coast. US Army adopted a defensive strategy, which had the objective of containing the enemy while gaining time needed to build base camps and logistical facilities. Operations as a part of this defensive strategy, which characterised US involvement until mid-1965, ultimately frustrated the efforts of the North Vietnamese and enabled the US military to consolidate positions from which to launch counteroffensives. Commensurate with the arrival of large numbers of US troops from mid-1965, General Westmoreland adopted a new strategy based on the belief that US forces, with their vastly superior weaponry and training, could defeat the enemy through the incremental attrition of their forces.

During this time, the United States also attempted to consolidate its ground operations more efficiently. For this purpose, it organised the US Army Vietnam (USARV). The I Corps tactical zone, composed of the five northernmost provinces, was to be primarily a Marine Corps responsibility; the US Army was to operate mainly in the II and III Corps tactical zones, which comprised the Central Highlands, adjacent coastal regions, and the area around Saigon; and formations of the Army of the Republic of Vietnam (ARVN) troops were to retain primary responsibility for the Delta region of the IV Corps.

Operation 'Highland'

After deploying to Vietnam at the end of July, the 1st Brigade of 101st Airborne was given precious little time to adjust to their new surroundings before commencing operations. The brigade was still without a home, as it had had no opportunity to establish a base camp, and was well on its way to earning the nick-name 'Nomads of Vietnam' that would endure throughout the war.

From 10 to 21 August the brigade conducted operations southwest of Nha Trang, and on 22 August moved north by sea and air to Binh Dinh Province, where it was to fight its first major action as part of Operation 'Highland'. The objective of 'Highland' was to secure a base at An Khe for the arrival of the 1st Air Cavalry Division (Airmobile). To allow the cavalry to debark safely, deploy to An Khe, and achieve a combat configuration, it was also essential to secure first Qui Nhon, second, Highway 19 connecting Qui Nhon and An Khe, and finally, An Khe itself.

NORTH VIETNAM

Theun

LAOS

Nakhon Phanom ●

Sakon Nakhon ●

Dong Hoi ●

DMZ

Dong Ha ●
Khe San ● Quang Tri ●
Tchepane ●

THAILAND

Mekong

Bang Hiene

Savannakhet ●

Muong Nong ●

Hue ●
● Phu Bai

Da Nang ●
Hoi An ●

POPULATION
Persons per square mile

⬜ 0–50
⬜ 50–250
⬜ 250–500
⬜ 500–750
⬜ 750 and over

Saravane ●

I CORPS

Tam Ky ●

Quang Ngai ●
● Mo Duc

Pakse ●

Attopeu ●

Dak To ●

● Hoa Nhon

Kontum ●

An Khe ●

Kong

San

Srepok

● Siem Reap

CAMBODIA

● Kompong Thom

● Hua Bon

Qui Nhon ●

Song Cau ●

● Tuy Hoa

II CORPS

● Ban Me Thuot

Pursat ●

Nha Trang ●

Kompong Cham ●

Gia Nghia ●

Da Lat ●

Phnom Penh ●

Mekong

Tay Ninh ●

Cu Chi ●

Takeo ●

Moc Hoa ●

Chau Phu ●

Ha Tien ●

IV CORPS

Bo Duc ●
Loc Ninh ●

An Loc ●

Phouc Vinh ●

III CORPS

Bien Hoa ●
● Xuan Loc

Saigon ●
Tan An ● ● Gia Dinh

My Tho ● Go Cong ●

● Phuoc Le

Bao Loc ●

● Phan Rhang

Phan Thiet ●

Han Tan ●

CAPITAL SPECIAL ZONE

Diong Dong ●

Rach Gia ●

● Can Tho

● Vi Thanh

Quan Long ●

● Vinh Loi

0 ————————— 100 MILES

0 ————————— 100 KILOMETRES

MAJOR OPERATIONS 1965–71

Operation	Location	Date
'Highland	Binh Dinh	Aug–Oct 1965
'Gibraltar	An Khe	Sept 1965
'Van Buren'	Tuy Hoa	Jan 1966
'Hawthorne'	Kontum	June 1966
'Paul Revere IV'	Chu Pong–Ia Drang	May–Dec 1966
'Wheeler'	Quang Nam–Quang Tri	Sept–Nov 1967
'Rose'	Phan Rang	Oct 1967
'Klamath Falls'	Song Mao/Bao Loc	Nov–Dec 1967
'Jeb Stuart'	Quang Tri	Jan–Mar 1968
'Carentan I'	Hue	March 1968
'Carentan II'	Hue	Apr–May 1968
(Lam Son 216)		
'Delaware'	A Shau Valley	Apr–May 1968
'Nevada Eagle'	Thua Thien Province	May–Aug 1968
(Lam Son 224)		
'Somerset Plain'	A Shau Valley	August 1968
'Kentucky Jumper'	Thua Thien Province	Mar–Aug 1969
'Massachusetts Striker'	A Shau Valley	Mar–May 1969
'Apache Snow'	A Shau Valley	May–June 1969
'Lamar Plain'	Tam Ky	May–Aug 1969
'Montgomery Rendezvous'	A Shau Valley	June–July 1969
'Saturate'	Thua Thien Province	Oct–Dec 1969
'Randolph Glen'	Thua Thien Province	Dec 1969–Mar 1970
'Texas Star'	Thua Thien Province	Apr 1969–Aug 1970
'Jefferson Glen'	Thua Thien Province	Sept 1970–Oct 1971
'Lam Son 719'	A Shau Valley/Laos	Mar–May 1971
'Lam Son 720'	A Shau Valley	Apr–Aug 1971

A task force designated 'Collins', consisting of the 2nd Battalion, 327th Infantry, moved overland from Cam Ranh Bay to Nha Trang and from there was airlifted to An Khe on the 24th of August. Between 22 and 25 August, all other elements of the brigade moved by truck from Cam Ranh Bay to Nha Trang, then by landing ship to Qui Nhon.

The initial landing at Qui Nhon was made by elements of the 1st Battalion, 327th Infantry, who along with 2nd Battalion, 502nd Infantry, assaulted west to clear Highway 19. This phase of Operation 'Highland' was successfully completed when a heliborne assault (Operation 'Talon') by the 1st Battalion, 327th Infantry, secured the critical An Khe pass – the same pass where previously the French Mobile Group 100 had been virtually annihilated.

Operation 'Gibraltar': Battle of Ah Ninh

Subsequently, a special task force was organised to secure convoy movement along Route 19 and establish strong points along the

Below: Pfc Jack Concannon, the chaplain's assistant, sets up an improvised altar during Operation 'Van Buren' on 23 January 1966. Note the M7 bayonet in its M8A1 scabbard attached to the shoulder of his M1956 load carrying equipment harness – obviously useful for dispensing communion wafers.

critical terrain bordering the route from Qui Nhon to the An Khe Pass. Tactical air cover was provided for all convoy traffic. While elements of the brigade guarded the 1st Cavalry Division's lifeline from Qui Nhon to An Khe, it also conducted eight airmobile assaults and many large ground operations to secure the division base area, utilising company-size or larger forces. These used a system of overlapping patrols and a series of sweeping operations designed to find, fix and destroy the enemy. Remarkably, there was no major loss of life or equipment due to enemy action in this period.

In mid-September one of these sweeps, dubbed Operation 'Gibraltar' and involving the 2nd Battalion, 502nd Infantry, and 1st Cavalry and 2nd Battalion, 320th Artillery, turned into the first major contact for the brigade and the first major battle for the US Army in Vietnam.

At 0700 hrs on 18 September, 26 Army UH-1 and Marine UH-34D helicopters landed all of C and part of B Companies of 2nd Battalion, 502nd Infantry, (some 224 men) near the village of An Ninh, almost nine miles north of Route 19. Upon landing, in what was later identified as a Viet Cong battalion command post, the troopers found themselves completely surrounded and outnumbered. Two of their 'slicks' were shot down. In the second wave, only half the choppers were able to set down on the landing zone (LZ). Most of the third wave was waved out of the area by a captain on the ground who was later killed, and even so it lost three helicopters to ground fire.

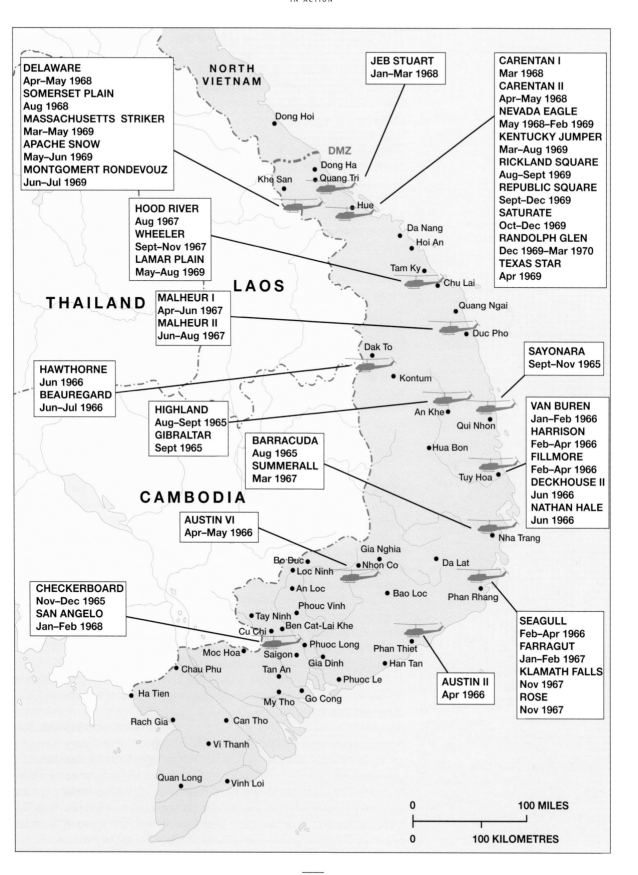

DELAWARE
Apr–May 1968
SOMERSET PLAIN
Aug 1968
MASSACHUSETTS STRIKER
Mar–May 1969
APACHE SNOW
May–Jun 1969
MONTGOMERT RONDEVOUZ
Jun–Jul 1969

JEB STUART
Jan–Mar 1968

CARENTAN I
Mar 1968
CARENTAN II
Apr–May 1968
NEVADA EAGLE
May 1968–Feb 1969
KENTUCKY JUMPER
Mar–Aug 1969
RICKLAND SQUARE
Aug–Sept 1969
REPUBLIC SQUARE
Sept–Dec 1969
SATURATE
Oct–Dec 1969
RANDOLPH GLEN
Dec 1969–Mar 1970
TEXAS STAR
Apr 1969

HOOD RIVER
Aug 1967
WHEELER
Sept–Nov 1967
LAMAR PLAIN
May–Aug 1969

MALHEUR I
Apr–Jun 1967
MALHEUR II
Jun–Aug 1967

HAWTHORNE
Jun 1966
BEAUREGARD
Jun–Jul 1966

HIGHLAND
Aug–Sept 1965
GIBRALTAR
Sept 1965

BARRACUDA
Aug 1965
SUMMERALL
Mar 1967

SAYONARA
Sept–Nov 1965

VAN BUREN
Jan–Feb 1966
HARRISON
Feb–Apr 1966
FILLMORE
Feb–Apr 1966
DECKHOUSE II
Jun 1966
NATHAN HALE
Jun 1966

AUSTIN VI
Apr–May 1966

CHECKERBOARD
Nov–Dec 1965
SAN ANGELO
Jan–Feb 1968

SEAGULL
Feb–Apr 1966
FARRAGUT
Jan–Feb 1967
KLAMATH FALLS
Nov 1967
ROSE
Nov 1967

AUSTIN II
Apr 1966

NORTH
VIETNAM

DMZ

LAOS

THAILAND

CAMBODIA

Dong Hoi

Khe San
Dong Ha
Quang Tri
Hue

Da Nang
Hoi An

Tam Ky
Chu Lai

Quang Ngai
Duc Pho

Dak To
Kontum

An Khe
Qui Nhon

Hua Bon

Tuy Hoa

Nha Trang

Gia Nghia
Nhon Co
Da Lat

Bo Duc
Loc Ninh
An Loc
Bao Loc
Phan Rhang

Phouc Vinh
Tay Ninh
Cu Chi
Ben Cat-Lai Khe

Moc Hoa
Saigon
Phuoc Long
Phan Thiet

Chau Phu
Tan An
Gia Dinh
Han Tan

Ha Tien
Phuoc Le

My Tho
Go Cong

Rach Gia
Can Tho

Vi Thanh

Quan Long
Vinh Loi

| 0 | | 100 MILES |
| 0 | | 100 KILOMETRES |

**101st AIRBORNE DIVISION
ORDER OF BATTLE
VIETNAM (1968)**

1st Brigade
    1st Battalion, 327th Infantry
    2nd Battalion, 327th Infantry
    2nd Battalion, 502nd Infantry

2nd Brigade
    1st Battalion, 501st Infantry
    2nd Battalion, 501st Infantry
    1st Battalion, 502nd Infantry

3rd Brigade
    (3rd Battalion, 506th Infantry)
    3rd Battalion, 187th Infantry
    1st Battalion, 506th Infantry
    2nd Battalion, 506th Infantry

101st Aviation Group
    101st Aviation Battalion
    158th Aviation Battalion
    159th Aviation Battalion
    163rd Aviation Company

    2nd Squadron, 17th Cavalry

101st Airborne Division Artillery
    4th Battalion, 77th Artillery
    2nd Battalion, 319th Artillery
    2nd Battalion, 320th Artillery
    1st Battalion, 321st Artillery

101st Military Police Company
326th Engineer Battalion
501st Signal Battalion
101st Airborne Division Support
    Command
101st Administration Company
326th Medical Battalion
426th Supply and Service Battalion
801st Maintenance Battalion
5th Transportation Battalion

Note: The 3rd Battalion, 506th Infantry was detached from the 101st Airborne Division from January 17th, 1968 to August 26th, 1970, during which period it was known as Task Force 3-506.

To compound the problem, 2nd Battalion of the 320th Artillery could not move its 105 mm guns into supporting position because of muddy roads, and had to wait until the evening for the 1st Cavalry's CH-47s Chinooks to airlift them into position.

By early the next morning, the supporting arms were in place and more infantry was inserted. As these reinforcements arrived, it became evident that the original assault had caught the enemy completely by surprise, and they were never able to reorganise their forces. Much of the credit must go to the surrounded troopers, who took the offensive and badly mauled the confused Viet Cong. When the battle ended three days later, 226 VC lay dead on the battlefield, bringing the number of enemy killed to date to 692, as against the 1st Brigade's losses of 21.

By the end of the month the 1st Cavalry had assumed responsibility for the An Khe area and the 101st was uprooted to Qui Nhon to provide security for the incoming Republic of Korea Capital ('Tiger') Division. In early November, the brigade at last established a base camp at Phan Rang, some 175 miles up the coast from Saigon. But except for a few hundred support troops inhabiting a corner of the base, Phan Rang was deserted for all but 21 days in two years, as the brigade moved to support operations around the country.

Battle of la Drang

Elsewhere, on 19 October 1965, three VC regiments totalling 6,000 men attacked a Civil Irregular Defense Group (CIDG)/US Special Forces camp at Plei Me, near the entrance to the la Drang Valley, in what purported to be the start of a thrust to cut the country in half. With the assistance of massive air strikes, elements of the newly arrived 1st Cavalry Division thwarted the enemy in a battle that lasted nearly a month and included several engagements. The la Drang Valley action was the costliest in terms of US casualties to date, yet the successful defence of the region improved security in and around the Central Highlands and raised the morale of the soldiers involved.

COUNTEROFFENSIVE

25 December 1965–30 June 1966

In December 1965 the United States again halted air attacks against North Vietnam, and invited the North Vietnamese government to negotiate an end to the fighting. The offer was refused. Ho Chi Minh's conditions for peace were clear cut. He demanded an end to the bombing and a complete American withdrawal. But withdrawal would mean almost certain defeat for the Republic of Vietnam, and its fall to Communism. President Johnson would not accept Ho's terms, and instead offered his own proposals, the most important of which was an immediate ceasefire between the belligerents. Neither side would compromise, however, and the fighting went on. In 1966 Johnson renewed the bombing attacks in North Vietnam, and also increased the number of US troops committed in the south.

Following the US victory in the la Drang Valley, American forces for the remainder of 1965 and well into 1966 sought to keep the enemy off balance while building base camps and logistical installations. This policy involved the use of search-and-destroy operations to protect the logistical bases under construction along the coast and the base camps for incoming US units in the provinces near Saigon.

Also of particular concern to the American military mission was the protection of the government and the people of South Vietnam. To these ends US efforts were concentrated in the most vital and heavily populated regions. The III Marine Amphibious Force supported the South Vietnamese I Corps in the northern provinces; I Field Force supported the Vietnamese II Corps in the central region; and II Field Force supported the South Vietnamese III Corps around Saigon. Consequently, the major battles of the year occurred in these critical areas.

Operation 'Van Buren'

Early in the new year, on 19 January, the 1st Brigade, 101st Airborne Division, the Korean 2nd Marine Brigade and the ARVN 47th Regiment began Operation 'Van Buren' to locate and destroy the PAVN 95th Regiment, which intelligence believed to be in the Tuy Hoa Valley. A second objective was to protect the rice harvest produced in the coastal region from seizure by the enemy.

Upon arriving at Tuy Hoa, the 1st Brigade moved straight into its operational areas. In the ensuing operation, 679 enemy casualties were verified. The 1st Brigade accounted for 282 enemy killed in action (KIA) plus 66 killed by artillery (KBA), 33 captured and 238 suspects detained. (The term killed-by-artillery was introduced a means of classifying enemy casualties for the statistics hungry Department of Defence.) Over 100 weapons, and several caches of ammo and supplies were also taken. The brigade's own casualties were 55 KIA and 221 WIA. During 20–23rd January, a temporary ceasefire was proclaimed in respect of the lunar new year (Tet), although minor clashes continued throughout this period.

Operation 'Hawthorne'

With the seasonal monsoon hampering air operations, spring 1966 passed relatively peacefully for the 1st Brigade. Then, in June, under the cover of rain and fog shrouding the Central Highlands, came a major PAVN offensive in Kontum Province. During this was fought the first battle of Dak To, a strategically important outpost in northern Kontum, which had been surrounded by units of the 24th PAVN Regiment. Against this a counterstrike – Operation 'Hawthorne' – was launched, to which the 1st Brigade was committed. While this succeeded in blunting the PAVN offensive in Kontum Province, it was to be a costly and hard-won victory.

Operation 'Hawthorne' began with a mission to rescue Vietnamese irregulars at the Tou Morong Special Forces Camp, near Dak To. The 1st Battalion of the 327th Infantry, commanded by Lt. Col. David H. Hackworth, and 1st Battalion of the ARVN's 42nd Regiment, were ordered to relieve it, and fought through moderate resistance to reach the hilltop garrison and evacuate the 150 inhabitants.

Hackworth then detached the 1st Battalion, 327th Infantry Regiment, to pursue the PAVN forces into the surrounding valleys. At 0230 hrs on the night of 6– 7 June, a battalion of the PAVN 24th Regiment counterattacked and partially overran the position held by Battery B, 2nd Howitzer Battalion (Airborne), 2nd Battalion of the 502nd Infantry, and Company A of the 226th Engineer Battalion in a valley west of Tou Morong. A major firefight broke out and raged until dawn, at which point the assaults halted. In a sweep of the area 86 enemy bodies were counted, 13 of them within the perimeter of the artillery position.

During the day, attacking north out of Tou Morong, one of the companies of the 1st Battalion, 327th Infantry, was badly mauled when it wandered into a PAVN base camp, and was saved only by artillery barrages and the insertion of additional infantry. It was now readily apparent to the officers directing the operation that a major PAVN force was present, and they sought an opportunity to destroy it. Companies of the 101st's 2nd battalion, 502nd Infantry, were quickly airlifted in to Dak To by C-130, from where they were to sweep south to aid the beleaguered force on the ground.

Dak To, in the heart of verdant jungle of the Central Highlands, is ringed on all sides by mountains, and behind those are yet taller ranges. 'I've never seen Dien Bien Phu,' one trooper remarked at the time, 'but this sure looks like the description.'

His apprehensions proved well founded; the ensuing battle (the first of a series that would be fought for control of the area) rapidly developed into one of the most viciously

Unit Headquarters (from 1967)

Bien Hoa Nov 67 - Feb 68
Bien Hoa/Phu Bai Mar 68 - Apr 69
Bien Hoa/Gia Le May 69 - Sept 69
Bien Hoa/Hue/Phu Bai Oct 69 - Nov 69
Hue/Phu Bai Dec 69 - Mar 72

1st 'Bastogne' Brigade - consisting of 1st and 2nd Battalion, 327th Infantry Regiment and 2nd Battalion, 502nd Infantry Regiment deployed to Vietnam from July 1965 to December 1971. Initially, the brigade operated out of Phan Rang, Ninh Thuan province, in II Corps Tactical Area of Responsibility (TAOR).

2nd 'Ready to Go' Brigade deployed to Vietnam between December 1967 and was originally based in the III Corps area, while the 1st Brigade continued operations in II Corps.

The 3rd Brigade was sent to the Dak To Highlands in mid-1968 and elements of that unit were later sent down to reinforce the 25th Infantry Division around Saigon. In September 1968, 3rd Brigade redeployed to I Corps at Phong Diem (just north of Camp Evans and south of Quang Tri). Although nominally a part of the brigade, 3rd Battalion, 506th Infantry operated out of Phan Thiet for most of the war and did not participate in any joint operations with any other elements of the 101st during the entire war. In May 1970, it was the only unit of the 101st to participate in the invasion of Cambodia.

On November 20th, 1971, 3rd Brigade redeployed to the United States and returned to its home at Fort Campbell.

Headquarters and Headquarters Company, 1st Brigade, 101st Airborne Division cited in Department of the Army General Orders 17, 23 April 1968, as amended by Department of the Army General Orders 1, 8 January 1969 (along with other attached units):

While participating in military operations: The 1st Brigade, 101st Airborne Division distinguished itself by extraordinary heroism from 17 January 1966 to 25 March 1966 while conducting Operations VAN BUREN and HARRISON against armed hostile forces in the vicinity of Tuy Hoa, Republic of Vietnam. After commencing Operation VAN BUREN on 17 January, the 1st Brigade deployed in the Tuy Hoa area to locate, fix, and destroy Viet Cong forces, while simultaneously protecting the local rice harvest from hostile seizure. The 1st Brigade not only defeated the insurgents decisively in four major battles, but also enabled the Vietnamese people to harvest a rice crop triple that of the previous year, when Viet Cong interference was unchecked. At Canh Tinh on 6 February, the 2d Battalion (Airborne), 502d Infantry killed 64 Viet Cong and completely routed a numerically superior force from heavily fortified emplacements. On the following day the 1st Battalion (Airborne), 327th Infantry took a toll of 66 insurgents in a savage conflict. During Operation HARRISON, that began on 21 February, the 1st Battalion (Airborne), 502d Infantry continued maneuvers in the Tuy Hoa area by searching out and destroying 118 of the enemy in a 5-hour pitched battle in the rice paddies around My Phu. After three days of difficult marching through mountainous jungle, the 2d Battalion (Airborne), 327th Infantry discovered a

contested actions of the Vietnam War. On the night of 7 June, human waves of the PAVN 24th Infantry Regiment surrounded and nearly overran the night laager of one of the companies. The company commander, an All-American football player at West Point named Captain William S. Carpenter, called in napalm strikes on his own position to repel the attack. While this earned him a citation for the Medal of Honor from General Westmoreland, some of his surviving men threatened to kill him.

Moving slowly from bunker to trench line, spider hole, bamboo thicket and stream bed the operation was nearing termination when tragedy struck. On 17 June a company of the 1st Battalion, 327th Infantry, engaged a small PAVN force in dense terrain. Responding to a call for support, 1st Cavalry helicopter gunships hit the company position itself.

But by the end of 'Hawthorne', the 24th PAVN Regiment had been all but destroyed. Hit by over 27,000 artillery rounds and 473 Air Force sorties, it suffered more than 1,200 dead and wounded, and the North Vietnamese offensive in Kontum was stopped dead in its tracks. US losses were more than 50 dead and 200 wounded.

As the 101st Airborne buried its dead, General Stanley R. Larsen, then commanding general of I Field Force, was moved to state publicly that the 1st Brigade was the 'best fighting unit in Vietnam'.

Battle of Truong Long

Even as Operation 'Hawthorne' was approaching its conclusion, another lesser-known but equally vicious action was about to be fought by the 101st Airborne in the Central Highlands. In early June, US Intelligence officers had identified a North Vietnamese unit of unknown size and location concentrated in the vicinity of Trung Luong. Fearing that these troops would attempt to take the US Special Forces base at nearby Dong Tre, II Corps called in the 1st Battalion, 5th Infantry (1st Cavalry Division), from An Khe and 2nd Battalion, 327th Infantry, from Tuy Hoah.

For these men, the remote hamlet of Truong Long was to become a name indelibly imprinted on their minds, and the battle fought there is acknowledged as one of the most brutal of the entire Vietnam War.

At the time the 2nd Battalion of 327th Infantry was commanded by Lt. Col. Joseph 'Wild Gypsy' Wasco, a 44-year-old veteran of the Second World War and the Korean War. At Trung Luong, working with the available intelligence, Wasco estimated he was faced by a battalion-strength unit in the order of 300 men. In fact, elements of three hardened North Vietnamese regiments were dug in around the hamlet – a force of some 3,000 to 4,000 men. Aerial reconnaissance missions did not detect the troops hidden in one of the most elaborate tunnel networks of the war, the fortified bunkers beneath ricestacks or the bunkers carved into the banks of winding creeks.

On the afternoon of 19 June 1966, A Company of the 2nd Battalion air-assaulted down toward the valley of Trung Luong. Just minutes after the 'slicks' touched down at the LZ, the company began taking casualties. Several paratroopers collapsed with heatstroke, overcome by stifling 100° temperatures and the smoke from burning bush grass, which had been set alight by artillery and helicopter gunships.

To make matters worse, the men were loaded like mules, typically carrying three days' worth of canned C rations, bandoliers of M-60 ammunition, their own M-16 rifles, extra ammo clips, claymore mines, grenades, clean socks, sleeping bags, ponchos, entrenching tools and two canteens of water per man.

The 139 men of A Company marched north with this load through the midday heat for almost three hours in the direction of Trung Luong. At nightfall, they halted and ambush patrols were sent out. Then at 0830 hrs the following morning, the company commander, Captain Tom Furgeson, got an urgent radio call from Wasco. The battalion's

C Company was pinned down by heavy enemy fire. Alpha Company was ordered to move west through Trung Luong to reinforce its sister company two miles away.

Furgeson led his company about a mile to a ridge finger known as Hill 48. He then sent a platoon, led by Lt. Walter Eddy, into the hamlet. As they approached, the air suddenly came alive with automatic fire and men began to drop wounded or dead to the ground. For 90 minutes A Company lay pinned down, before Furgeson was compelled to radio for permission to pull back to the ridge and call in air strikes. The survivors marched back up the ridge, exhausted, and watched as Navy aircraft laced the hamlet with napalm. From his command post on the ridge finger, Furgeson radioed Wasco again. C Company still desperately needed help. Both officers agreed: A Company had to go back into Trung Luong.

Early that same afternoon, 20 June, B Company was preparing to assault into a LZ atop Hill 258, just northwest of Trung Luong. The company had been yanked from another battle and ordered to take the hill, then link up with A and C Companies. As the Hueys touched down on Hill 258, they came down slightly off the intended landing zone, into a swarm of enemy fire. By the time the last chopper landed, at about 1500 hrs, dead and wounded littered the ridge top, but by daybreak on 21 June, the position was taken.

Back at Hill 48, Furgeson had taken A Company back down into Trung Luong shortly after 1400 hrs on 20 June. As the men approached down a dry creek bed the PAVN troops opened fire from bunkers set in the creek bank. The firefight was still raging when a helicopter brought in Colonel Hal Moore, a brigade commander with the First Cavalry, who now assumed command of the situation.

A Company's wounded were loaded onto choppers. The remainder – tired, thirsty, some sick with dysentery and all of them scared – went back into the hamlet on the morning of 21 June. This time, as they approached the hedgerow where they had been ambushed the day before, most were certain they going to die. Another fierce firefight erupted, but in the face of fresh reinforcements, during the night the enemy began to melt away. By the next morning, they had evacuated. There was only scattered resistance as A and C Companies came within sight of one another in Trung Luong, now deserted. A Company pulled back for the final time, bringing out its casualties.

In the aftermath of the battle, some 371 enemy dead were counted on the battlefield. US commanders estimated the full figure to be nearer 400. Although the remainder of 24th PAVN Regiment managed to escape into Laos, North Vietnamese battle reports reveal that it had been seriously mauled. In them, PAVN officers speak of hunger, malaria, desertions, sleep deprivation and shell-shock (118 tons of napalm, 107 tons of bombs and 26,000 artillery rounds had been directed at them) among their men.

A Company had also suffered grievously. In truth, it had been virtually annihilated. Of the 139 men who had gone in on 19 June, plus two dozen reinforcements, only 42 were still standing. More than 70 had been killed or wounded, and dozens more had been felled by heat stroke. (The PAVN claimed it had killed 144 Americans.)

The Fields of Bamboo, an account of Trung Luong and two other battles by US Army historian S.L.A. Marshall has this to say. 'Few, if any, United States rifle companies in the Vietnam War were more sorely tried.'

Other operations

During 1966 there were 18 major operations, the most successful of these being Operation 'White Wing' (originally named 'Masher' and sometimes referred to as the 'Bong Son Campaign'). Launched on 24 January, 'Masher' was the first major search-and-destroy operation of the Vietnam War. It entailed a 42-day sweep over 2,000 square miles of forested mountains and rugged valleys by the 1st Cavalry Division, Korean Capitol Division and ARVN 22nd Division in northern Binh Dinh Province in II Corps

Viet Cong regimental headquarters. The men fiercely broke the hostile defenses that were in a nearly impregnable cave complex and uncovered one of the largest caches captured in the counterinsurgency efforts. While suffering only light casualties in both operations, the 1st Brigade killed more than 500 Viet Cong, wounded hundreds more and captured nearly 500 insurgents and suspects. Not content with merely defeating the enemy, the men of this exceptional unit strengthened the safety and health of the local Vietnamese population by tireless efforts in medical treatment, road building and protection of the valuable rice crop. Their extensive military and civic accomplishments deeply depressed enemy morale and struck an irreparable blow to insurgency efforts in the vicinity of Tuy Hoa. The extraordinary heroism and devotion to duty displayed by the men of the 1st Brigade, 101st Airborne Division, were in keeping with the highest traditions of the military service and reflect distinct credit upon themselves and the Armed Forces of the United States.

The 1st Brigade, 101st Airborne Division
(Airmobile) and attached units
distinguished themselves by extraordinary
heroism in action against a hostile force in
Dak To, Republic of Vietnam, during
Operation 'Hawthorne', 2 through 20 June
1966. 'Hawthorne' began on 2 June 1966
when the Brigade was directed to relieve
the beleaguered mountain outpost of Tou
Morong. The 1st Battalion (Airborne),
327th Infantry teamed up with elements of
the 24th Tactical Zone Command (42d
Army of the Republic of Vietnam Regiment
and the 21st Ranger Battalion) to
accomplish this phase of the operation.
Intelligence reports received at Brigade
Headquarters indicated a major enemy
drive was under way to overrun the Central
Highlands. At 0230 hours on the morning
of 7 June 1966, and estimated North
Vietnamese battalion of the 24th North
Vietnamese Army Regiment savagely
attacked an artillery position in the valley
west of Tou Morong. The position was
manned by Battery B, 2d Howitzer Battalion
(Airborne), 320th Artillery; Company A, 2d
Battalion (Airborne), 502d Infantry; and
elements of Company A, 326th Engineer
Battalion. The charging enemy was able to
penetrate the artillery's perimeter. The
battle that had the winner-take-all climax
saw the valiant Americans secure their
weapons and fire point-blank into the still
charging North Vietnamese Army ranks.
As dawn brought light to the exhausted
warriors, 86 enemy bodies were counted,
13 of them inside the artillery position.
After relieving the Tou Morong outpost, the
1st Battalion (Airborne), 327th Infantry,
moved north. Another bitter battle erupted,
this time engaging all three of the infantry

Tactical Zone. In the process they decimated a division, later established as the North Vietnamese 3rd Division. The operation ended on 6 March.

Running concurrent with 'Masher', Marine Corps and ARVN units working with the 1st Cavalry Division (Airmobile) made an unsuccessful attempt to trap PAVN and VC units in the Tam Quan region of Quang Ngai Province in a pincer envelopment: Operation 'Double Eagle'.

Also during February and March, US intelligence reported heavy North Vietnamese Army infiltration from Laos and across the demilitarised zone into Quang Tri Province. The US 3rd Marine Division was moved into the area of the two northern provinces to operate in concert with the ARVN 1st Division and 173rd Airborne Brigade. On 12 April, US B-52s based on Guam bombed infiltration routes near the Laos border, in the first use of these bombers against PAVN troops. These actions succeeded in driving the PAVN back, forcing it to take refuge in Laos, Cambodia and North Vietnam; they temporarily removed the threat of harassment to the populace by North Vietnamese regular forces and curbed local guerrilla activity.

COUNTEROFFENSIVE, PHASE II

1 July 1966–31 May 1967

During this period the American military establishment in Vietnam grew ever larger. The elaborate system of base camps continued to be developed, ports and airports were built or improved, and massive logistical support was provided. By 3 December 1966 US military personnel in South Vietnam numbered 385,300, and by 30 June 1967 this number had risen to 448,800.

Allied operations after 1 July 1966 were by and large a continuation of the earlier counteroffensive campaign. The Joint Chiefs of Staff declared that American military objectives should be to cause North Vietnam to cease its control and support of the insurgency in South Vietnam and Laos, to assist South Vietnam in defeating Viet Cong and North Vietnamese forces in the country, and to assist South Vietnam in pacification and extending governmental control over its territory.

However, the essence of Communist control over the populace – the VC infrastructure in the hamlets and villages – remained essentially unaffected as the pacification programme failed to make significant headway. At the same time, North Vietnam continued to build its own forces inside South Vietnam; their total strength was in excess of 282,000 in addition to an estimated 80,000 political cadres.

Infiltration was first routed by sea and along the Ho Chi Minh trail and then, in early 1967, through the demilitarised zone (DMZ). US air elements received permission to conduct reconnaissance bombing raids and tactical air strikes into North Vietnam just north of the DMZ, but ground forces were denied authority to conduct reconnaissance patrols in the northern portion of the zone or inside North Vietnam. Confined to South Vietnamese territory, US ground forces were forced to fight a war of attrition, relying for a time on body counts as one standard indicator for measuring successful progress in the conduct of the war.

Operation 'Paul Revere IV'

From May to December 1966, Allied units were heavily engaged in screening operations along the Cambodian border in the northeastern sector of II Corps, under the operational designation 'Paul Revere'. 'Paul Revere IV' (18 October–30 December) was a major search-and-destroy operation along the border, conducted primarily by the newly arrived 4th Infantry Division in conjunction with the 1st Cavalry Division. It was centred on the Chu Pong–Ia Drang area. When it became clear that the enemy was attempting to withdraw into Laos, a massive helicopter airlift of the 1st Brigade, 101st Airborne Division, was staged, but the brigade was landed just as the enemy was crossing into Laos and safety. 'Paul Revere IV' was declared officially concluded on 30th December, and the brigade was subsequently ordered into reserve in Phu Yen Province.

During the early part of 1967, the brigade was used as a rapid reaction force, reinforcing American and South Vietnamese forces when necessary and responding to enemy attacks. In April, the brigade was attached to Task Force Oregon, placed under operational control of the III Marine Amphibious Force and moved to Chu Lai on the eastern coast. Task Force Oregon was a multi-brigade army force, organised by Major General William Rosson, and composed of the 196th Light Infantry Brigade, 1st Brigade of 101st Airborne, and the 3rd Brigade of 25th Infantry Division. At Chu Lai, it assisted in operations to blunt an offensive by the PAVN 2nd Division and to enable units of the 3rd Marine Task Force to relocate to Quang Tri province. Later, it was called in to assist a Marine battalion in beating off an enemy attack around Khe Sanh, to where it would return in the long, bloody siege of 1968. Also in April, the 3rd Battalion (Airborne), 506th Infantry, was reactivated at Fort Campbell under Lt. Col. John P. Geraci.

Other operations

In November 1966 a major sweep – Operation 'Attleboro' – was undertaken in the so-called 'Iron Triangle' area (War Zone C) about 25 miles northwest of Saigon. For years this area had been under development as a VC logistics base and headquarters to control enemy activity in and around Saigon. Some 22,000 US and ARVN troops were pitted against the VC 9th Division and a PAVN regiment. Several pitched battles occurred between the opposing forces, the most significant at Ap Cha Do, before the PAVN/VC fled over the border to safe havens in Cambodia or Laos. Generally, 'Attleboro' was a success, destroying the 9th VC Division's extensive base area and reducing its effectiveness for about six months. Furthermore, it demonstrated that large numbers of battalions could arrive quickly in an operational area and bring the enemy to battle, thus setting the scene for subsequent large scale operations: 'Cedar Falls' and 'Junction City'.

On 8 January 1967, US and South Vietnamese troops launched further drives against two major VC strongholds in the Iron Triangle, under Operation 'Cedar Falls'. The Allies captured caches of rice and other foodstuffs, destroyed an elaborate system of tunnels, and seized documents of major intelligence value.

Following a little over a month after 'Cedar Falls', on 22 February these same US forces were committed with other units in the largest allied operation of the war to date: Operation 'Junction City'. The primary objective of this corps-sized action was the elimination of the Viet Cong 9th Division in War Zone C. Some 22 US and four ARVN battalions engaged the enemy, but by the time 'Junction City' terminated on 14 May they had not been unable to decisively neutralise the area. The operation did, however, convince the Communists to move their headquarters into Cambodia and out of reach of Allied forces.

COUNTEROFFENSIVE, PHASE III

1 June 1967–29 January 1968

From midway through 1967 until early in the new year, efforts aimed at 'Vietnamisation' of the conflict, so that the armed forces of the Republic of Vietnam could assume greater responsibility for operations against North Vietnam, were

companies of the Battalion at one time, each in a separate fire fight. As the battle raged, the Battalion's elite Tiger Force was hard hit and almost overrun by an estimated two companies of heavily armed, well trained North Vietnamese Army Regulars. On 7 June 1966, the 2d Battalion (Airborne), 502d Infantry, was helilifted into a blocking position where it began a sweep south to link up with its heavily engaged sister Battalion. Throughout the battle, the enemy strength was fixed as a well trained North Vietnamese Army Regiment. Their heavy weapons were strategically placed in sturdy bunkers which were spread out along the fingers and draws of mountainside. As the battered but courageous 2d Battalion (Airborne), 502d Infantry companies regrouped and the 1st Battalion (Airborne), 327th Infantry, continued their relentless attack from the south, a decision was made to have B-52 Bombers strike Dak Tan Kan Valley before the Brigade moved in for the final kill. 'Hawthorne' was one of the most viciously contested battles of the Vietnam War. Day and Night the battle raged, moving from bunker to trench line, to spider hole, to bamboo thicket, to stream bed, and finally to victory. At the conclusion of 'Hawthorne' the 24th North Vietnamese Army Regiment was rendered ineffective as a fighting unit, suffering 1200 casualties by body count and estimate. By comparison, friendly casualties were 48 dead and 239 wounded. A major North Vietnamese offensive to seize the North Central Highlands was blunted. Throughout 'Hawthorne' the extraordinary heroism, dogged determination, gallantry, and indomitable spirit with which the 1st Brigade, 101st Airborne Division, successfully accomplished all assigned missions were in keeping with the finest traditions of the United States Army and reflect great credit upon all members of the Brigade who participated in this remarkable combat action.

Above: Lt Daniel Hill of Company B, 2nd Battalion, 327th Infantry (Airborne), 1st Brigade, 101st Airborne Division (Separate), sets fire to a village hut during Operation 'Van Buren' on 23 January 1966. Operation 'Van Buren' was conducted in Phu Yen Province to deny the local rice harvest to the VC/NVA. Such acts did much to alienate US forces from the rural population who were caught between the fear of intimidation from the communists and the lack of security provided by the Saigon government. For the average peasant farmer, it was a no-win situation.

increasingly realised. Vietnamese Special Forces assumed responsibility for several Special Forces camps and for the CIDG companies manning them. In each case all of the US advisors withdrew, leaving the Vietnamese in full command. With an increased delegation of responsibility to them, the South Vietnamese conducted major operations during 1967 and, in spite of VC attempts to avoid battle, achieved a number of contacts.

The number of US troops in Vietnam continued to increase. In August 1967, the remainder of the 101st Airborne Division was alerted for deployment to Vietnam from Fort Campbell, two years and 27 days after the departure of the 1st Brigade.

Throughout this period the nature of operations in South Vietnam remained basically unchanged. In II Corps, as Operation 'Junction City' ended, elements of the US 1st and 25th Infantry Divisions, the 11th Armored Cavalry Regiment and the forces of the Army of the Republic of Vietnam swung back toward Saigon to conduct another clearing operation – 'Manhattan' – conducted in the Long Nguyen base area just north of Iron Triangle.

Operation 'Wheeler'

In I Corps TAOR, following on from Task Force Oregon, Operation 'Wheeler' was launched in Quang Nam and Quang Tin Provinces on 11 September 1967. During this operation the 1st Brigade encountered elements of the 2nd PAVN Division west of Tam Ky, and used surprise airmobile assaults into the Song Tranh Valley to flush them out. The fleeing PAVN were killed in droves. After three weeks close to 400 had been killed, and by early November this had more than doubled, making 'Wheeler' the largest single operation conducted by the brigade in Vietnam to date. By the time it was concluded after 75 days, the 1st Brigade troopers had killed 1,105 enemy. With 'Wheeler' successfully concluded, the 1st Brigade was detached from the Americal Division to prepare for the arrival of 2nd and 3rd Brigades and support elements. (The Americal or 23rd Infantry Division had been formed from the former Task Force Oregon, to which the 1st Brigade was still seconded, Shortly after the operation commenced.)

On 26 October, the USNS *General Weigel* arrived at Cam Ranh Bay carrying the 3rd Battalion (Airborne), 506th Infantry. The troops disembarked at 1030 hrs and then moved to Phan Rang base camp in II Corps: the 'Eagle's Roost'. Soon after arrival they began 'P-training' (Proficiency School), while two groups of battalion officers and NCOs went to Chu Lai (I Corps) for 'on-the-job' training with their counterparts in the 1st Brigade.

Between 11 and 30 November the battalion engaged in Operation 'Rose', its first combat operation. 'Rose', a combination search-and-destroy and reconnaissance-in-force mission was conducted southwest of Phan Rang. Although the primary mission was to find, fix, and destroy Viet Cong/NVA forces and to neutralise their base camps, especially Secret Base 35, it was also designed to provide security for engineers working on Highway QL 1 (Route 1). Assaulting into a hot LZ the battalion's B Company, under Captain Landgraf, made the first contact with the enemy, the Viet Cong's 112th and C-270 Local Force Companies. Over the ensuing two weeks the battalion skirmished with enemy units on almost a daily basis. By the time the operation ended on 30 November (Thanksgiving Day), eight NVA/Viet Cong were confirmed KIA. US casualties were nine WIA.

Late in November, the 1st Brigade moved back to the divisional base camp at Phan Rang after an eight-month deployment to I Corps. In the two and a half years since arriving, the unit had made 31 tactical deployments, travelling more than 2,500 miles to conduct 25 major operations in three of the four tactical zones. The troopers accounted for 6,000 enemy killed, captured enough weapons to equip eight enemy battalions, and took 2,000 tons of rice. Medical treatment was provided for more than 25,000 Vietnamese, and more than 15,000 refugees were relocated. Four thousand miles of road were cleared of enemy control.

Below: Capt. Dennis Anderson, the Intelligence Officer of the 2nd Battalion, 502nd Infantry (Airmobile), 101st Airborne Division (Separate), listens as an ARVN officer interrogates a VC suspect during Operation 'Cook', a search and destroy mission in the mountains of Quang Ngai Province on 7 September 1967. At this time, the 1st Brigade was part of Task Force Oregon, a division-sized US Army formation that was created from several different units to allow the US Marines in Quang Ngai Provinve to redeploy to the DMZ area in strength. Task Force Oregon operated between April and September 1967 when it was superseded by the 23rd Infantry Division (Americal).

Operation 'Klamath Falls'

After refitting at Phan Rang, an advance party of the 3rd Battalion, 506th Infantry, moved by helicopter to Song Mao in preparation for a new operation: 'Klamath Falls'. Following the current pattern of US Army operations, 'Klamath Falls' was a combination search-and-destroy and reconnaissance-in-force mission. The primary objective was to seek out and destroy the headquarters of the enemy's MR-6 (Military Region 6) and all enemy forces in the area of operations – Binh Thuan and Lam Dong Provinces – including the PAVN/Viet Cong 146th, 186th, 482nd, and 840th Main Force Viet Cong Battalions. Another operational objective was to open and keep open Highway QL-1 from the II Corps boundary to the Binh Thuan–Ninh Thuan Province boundary.

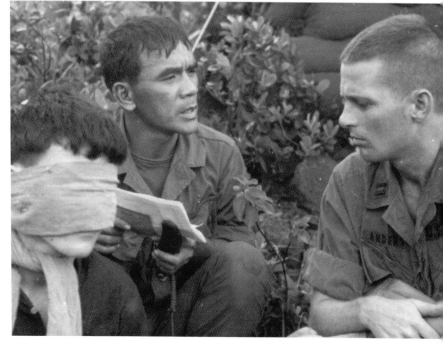

Under 'Klamath Falls', 3rd Battalion operated for the first time with its parent unit: the 1st Brigade, 101st Airborne Division. Also involved were elements of the 2nd Battalion of the 7th Cavalry, 1st Cavalry Division, based at Phan Thiet, the 23rd ARVN Division and Company B of the 5th Special Forces Group. The 'Currahees' (the 'Stand Alone' 3rd Battalion of the 506th Infantry) joined the battle on 3 December and were soon in the thick of the fighting. During the night of the 8th the three Montagnard Popular Forces (PF) platoons guarding the hamlet of Tahine were overrun and destroyed by the 186th Main Force VC Battalion armed with mortars, machine guns, and rocket launchers. A relief force from 3rd Battalion, 506th Infantry, was ordered in, but met with heavy opposition.

After more than two weeks of heavy fighting, at 1800 hrs on Christmas Eve, a temporary ceasefire became effective, allowing the men to make the best of their Christmas away from home. Although all Battalions of the 1st Brigade ceased search-and-destroy operations, rifle companies continued to conduct security patrolling activities in their immediate areas. All too briefly, at 1800 hrs on Christmas Day, the ceasefire agreement ended and normal operations resumed. Over the New Year, there was another brief hiatus in respect of the new year.

Other operations

In the autumn of 1967 there were indications of another enemy build-up, particularly in areas close to Laos and Cambodia. In late October, the VC struck again at the Special Forces Camp at Loc Ninh, but

Above: The location of the 1st Brigade of 101st Airborne during the period July 1965–June 1967..

the timely intervention of South Vietnamese reinforcements saved the position. At the same time, approximately 12,000 VC troops converged on the Special Forces camp at Dak To, in northern Kontum Province. In response to these threats, the US and South Vietnam committed a total of 16 battalions to the region.

Operation 'Eagle Lift'

As the year drew to an end, the 2nd and 3rd Brigades of the 101st Airborne Division arrived in Vietnam to bring the division up to its full strength and enable it to convert to a full airmobile division. Originally, the deployment was scheduled for 10 February 1968, but this movement was brought forward to December. The culmination of the division's preparations was Operation 'Eagle Thrust' – the largest and longest military airlift ever attempted into a combat zone. Ending on 18 December, it brought 10,024 troops and over 5,300 tons of the division's essential equipment to Bien Hoa Air Base in 369 C-141 Starlifter missions and 22 C-133 Cargomaster missions.

Once in country, division headquarters was set up at Bien Hoa; the 2nd Brigade established an area of operation (AO) around Cu Chi. Next they moved to Phuoc Vinh to prepare a base camp for the 3rd Brigade. Prior to commencing operations the troopers went through a 30-day in-country training programme designed by the 25th Infantry, receiving daily instruction on booby traps, reconnaissance and explosives. Small-unit leaders who lacked combat experience accompanied elements of the 25th Infantry on search and destroy missions.

With the temporary cease fire ended on 1 January, 3rd Battalion, 506th Infantry, continued its operations in Bao Loc. On 2nd, a platoon of the battalion ran into a large, dug-in Viet Cong force at the knoll on Di Linh Plateau southeast of Bao Loc. The ensuing 'Battle of the Knoll' raged into the night, resulting in the loss of six men KIA and another 20 wounded. On the following day reinforcements in the form of the battalion's Alpha Company arrived, and over the next five days the platoon skirmished with the enemy and uncovered numerous enemy sites, bunker complexes, base camps, weapons, medical supply caches, hospitals, mess halls and graves. These finds were significant enough to have I Field Force commander, General William B. Rosson, and 1st Brigade commander, Brigadier General S.H. Matheson, visit the field sites.

On 8th 'Klamath Falls' was terminated. Task force elements were extracted from the area of operations to the battalion LZ along Highway QL-20 to prepare for a motor convoy move to Phan Rang on 9 January. Battalion losses for the operation were 10 KIA and 34 WIA.

In the middle of the month, the battalion received an unexpected order to make ready for a combat jump into an NVA Division Headquarters northwest of Song Be, scheduled for 1000 hrs, 17 January 1968. The men dutifully began preparations for this mission. It was all in vain; at the last moment, word came from General Westmoreland that due to a security violation the jump was cancelled.

Above: 101st Airborne deployments in Vietnam December 1967–March 1972.

They moved instead to Phan Thiet in Binh Thuan Province, located in II Corps area, and assumed responsibility for AO Byrd – covering the four southern provinces of Ninh Thuan, Binh Thuan, Tuyen Duc and Dam Dong – from the departing 1st Cavalry Division (Airmobile). At Phan Thiet the 3rd Battalion, 506th Infantry, became the nucleus of an airborne-airmobile task force under the operational control of the commander, First Field Force Vietnam (I FFORCEV). On 20th Task Force 3/506 initiated Operation 'McLain', an open-end search-and-destroy operation that ran for a little over a year in AO Byrd, as well as in portions of Binh Tuy Province in III Corps. As with all other US offensive operations, this was halted on 29 January for the upcoming three-day celebration of the Vietnamese lunar New Year (Tet) for 1968 beginning on 30 January.

TET/TET COUNTEROFFENSIVE

30 January 1968–1 April 1968

In 1968, however, Tet did not pass in its customary peace. In fact it was marked by the biggest PAVN/VC offensive of the war thus far. Between 30 January and the end of

February 1968, some 84,000 VC and North Vietnamese attacked or fired upon 36 of 44 provincial capitals, five of six autonomous cities, 64 of 242 district capitals and 50 hamlets, extending from Khe Sanh in the north to Ca Mau on the country's southern tip. In addition, the enemy raided a number of military installations, including almost every airfield. Perhaps most daring though was the attack at the very heart of the US administration: its embassy in Saigon.

Now known as the Tet Offensive, this operation was timed to coincide with the beginning of Tet, an annual celebration of the lunar New Year, and the most festive of Vietnamese holidays. Planned by PAVN General Vo Nguyen Giap, the objective was to stimulate an popular uprising (*khoi nghia*), a means that the Vietnamese had previously employed to overthrow oppressors.

Determined enemy assaults began in the northern and Central provinces before daylight on 30 January, and in Saigon and the Mekong Delta regions that night. The first wave of assaults lasted three days, and Saigon and Hue came under the most intense and sustained attack. Although most incursions were crushed in a few days, fighting continued in some areas for up to two months. Collectively, it was the bloodiest phase of the entire war. North Vietnam lost 50,000 soldiers killed, South Vietnam 14,000 and the US 2,000. In addition, an estimated 12,500 civilians were killed, and Tet created as many as a million new refugees.

Below: Men of the 4th Platoon, Company C, 1st Battalion, 327th Infantry (Airmobile), 1st Brigade, 101st Airborne Division (Airmobile), cross a river by means of a rope strung from bank to bank during Operation 'San Angelo' on 20 January 1968. The numerous waterways and paddy fields of Vietnam often made progress across the countryside a slow and painful process with the constant fear of ambush or bobby traps.

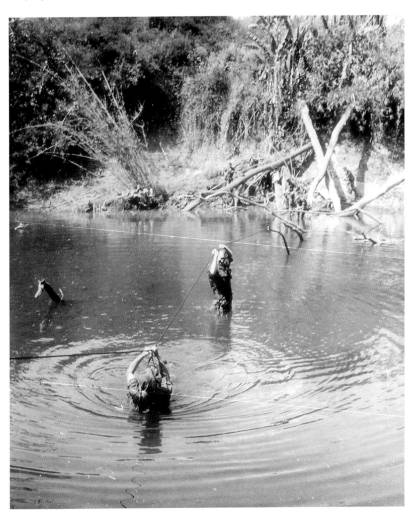

As it turned out, the PAVN suffered a heavy military defeat, but Tet is widely seen as an enormous psychological and propaganda victory for North Vietnam. It came as a profound shock to the US public, which up to that time had been fed greatly exaggerated claims by the military establishment about the efficacy of the US-led campaign, and led to believe that the North Vietnamese were a largely spent force. Tet did irreparable damage to public confidence in the politicians and soldiers running the Vietnam War.

It was no less of a shock to the troops, as previously both sides had observed a ceasefire during Tet. Hence the American forces and their South Vietnamese allies, relaxing and celebrating as in years past, were caught completely off guard. At the time all eyes were focused instead on an isolated Marine Corps outpost strategically sited near the Laotian border and DMZ in the far northwestern corner of South Vietnam: Khe Sanh.

Khe Sanh

Ten days prior to the opening attacks, three PAVN divisions had begun probing attacks on the perimeter of Khe Sanh, part of a network of interconnected bases along the DMZ, envisaged by General Westmoreland as a barrier to enemy infiltration. US staff officers had been predicting a major assault on Khe Sanh for some time, and recent intelligence seemed to confirm this. General Giap, the North Vietnamese commander, had in fact gathered close to 30,000 experienced troops in the area, and beginning on 20 January they laid siege to Khe Sanh for over six weeks. With memories of the French debacle at Dien Bien Phu not far from their thoughts, President Johnson and Westmoreland ordered massive resources to be funnelled into the effort to save the base. It was held at huge cost in men and materiel, only to be abandoned in the summer.

Whether the attack on Khe Sanh was intended to act as a decoy for the main offensive is still debated, but there is no question that the US forces were caught off guard.

Above: Men of the 327th Infantry (Airborne), 1st Brigade, 101st Airborne Division (Separate), come ashore from an LST – Tank Landing Ship – as part of a search and destroy operation conducted by Task Force Oregon in May 1967 in the Duc Pho district of Quang Ngai Province. Although qualified paratroopers, the troopers of the 101st Airborne Division deployed into battle by any means during the long and frustrating war in Vietnam in their attempts to find and eliminate the elusive enemy.

This was certainly true at Bien Hoa, headquarters of the 101st Airborne, where one of the biggest attacks fell. Although the divisional intelligence had known of the enemy build-up at the Bien Hoa–Saigon area prior to the beginning of Tet, they had no idea of when or where an attack might come, and like other units the 101st Airborne was observing the 36-hour ceasefire. At around 0300 hrs on 31 January an assault began at the main gate of the installation, within sight of the headquarters building itself. The 2nd Battalion, 506th Airborne Infantry, was quickly flown in by helicopter from Phuoc Vinh and within a half hour was fighting a pitched battle. In the next seven hours, more than 100 enemy fell, and another 58 the next day, 1 February.

Battle of the Embassy

Also on 31 January, a dramatic battle was fought by troopers of C Company, 3rd Platoon, 1st Battalion, 502nd Airborne Infantry, at the US Embassy in Saigon.

In the early hours of the morning the division commander, Major General O.M. Barsanti, received a message requesting a reinforcing element for the forces under attack at the US Embassy in Saigon. A 35-man reaction force, led by Major Hillel Schwartz, assistant division intelligence officer, was quickly assembled. Schwartz gave a quick appraisal of the situation to his men; Marines were barricaded in the Embassy; military police units were on the outside perimeter of the courtyard and Viet Cong armed with automatic weapons and rocket-propelled grenade (RPG) launchers were inside the embassy itself.

At 0633 hrs, Schwartz, Captain Speedy and two sergeants boarded a helicopter and flew to Saigon. Flying over the city, they observed gun battles all over, and particularly in the area of the embassy. As it came into land on the embassy roof, the helicopter began to take hits from small arms, wounding the door gunner in the hand and shoulder. The chopper was forced to pull away, with Schwartz returning fire at the muzzle flashes below with the M-16 rifle he had hastily poked out the door.

The pilot, Lt. Col. John McGregor, commander of the 101st Aviation Battalion, noted that the aircraft was overheating and recommended they divert to Long Binh, where the wounded gunner could be hospitalised and another chopper could be obtained. With this accomplished they took off again for the embassy, and this time got in without taking any hits. After searching the roof, the team moved to the ground floor using the elevator.

Above: Men of the 1st Battalion, 327th Infantry (Airmobile), 1st Brigade, 101st Airborne Division (Airmobile), pick up rolls of concertina wire dropped by helicopter to bolster the perimeter defences of Fire Support Base Saber.

Everywhere the walls were peppered with bullet holes, and out in the courtyard MPs were pursuing Viet Cong dressed in civilian clothes and carrying AK-47 assault rifles.

Schwartz ordered the area to be methodically swept, and when this had been done 19 bodies littered the ground, some lying sprawled among the big flower planters. While the paratrooper platoon secured the area, the bodies were searched for captured documents and weapons.

With the embassy compound restored to US control, General Westmoreland arrived and was accompanied by Schwartz on an inspection of the courtyard. As the two looked at the big hole blown in the embassy wall, the general was called to the phone. It was a call from the President in Washington, anxious to know what was happening.

Battle for Hue: Operation 'JEB Stuart'

But it was in and around Hue, the ancient former Imperial capital of Vietnam, that the bitterest and bloodiest battle of the Tet Offensive was fought. In the early hours of 31 January, the 6th PAVN Regiment and 12th VC Sapper Battalion stormed the old Imperial Citadel on the northern bank of the Perfume River, while the 4th PAVN Regiment attacked the Military Assistance Command Vietnam (MACV) compound on the south bank. By dawn most of the city, and large parts of the Quang Tri/Thua Thien area north of Hue was in communist hands. Although ARVN and Marine units launched immediate counterattacks to recapture the city, the citadel was only retaken on 24 February.

Shortly after the opening attacks on Hue, C-130 transport aircraft carried the 2nd Brigade 500 miles north to I Corps. En route, it stopped first at Phu Bai Airport then bivouacked briefly at nearby LZ El Paso (later to become Camp Eagle), a 1st Cavalry Division firebase, before joining operations with the Cavalry in the vicinity of Quang Tri. On 2 February, anticipating that the Viet Cong and North Vietnamese would attempt to withdraw to the west, and in order to prevent reinforcements from reaching those PAVN units already inside the city, the 3rd Brigade, 1st Cavalry, and 1st Battalion of the 501st Infantry established blocking positions to the west. Units of the 1st Cavalry and elements of the 101st Division also attacked south along QL-1 (Highway 1) and toward the northern quadrants of Hue City.

Initial contact with the enemy in the Battle for Hue occurred near the village of Van Xa/PK 17, which was part of an area known generally as the 'Street Without Joy' (and which later became the site of LZ Sally, adjacent to the village of Van Xa) a little over six miles northwest of Hue. At about the time these elements fought through to the northern outskirts of Hue City itself, the enemy broke contact and fled north, west and east to avoid annihilation.

By 9 February, Marines had fought from house to house to clear the south bank of the Perfume River. On the north bank the action was similarly intense, but movement was slower and it wasn't until the 21st that a combined Marine/ARVN force managed to link up with the 1st Cavalry moving from the west. On 9 March, after completing their phase of the operation, 2nd Brigade rejoined the division.

Although the battles on the outskirts of Hue are largely ignored, former airborne troopers are quick to point out that during Operation 'JEB Stuart' the army took more casualties in one week than the Marines lost in their very famous and well-publicised month-long fight to liberate Hue (attacking from the south).

COUNTEROFFENSIVE, PHASE IV

2 April–30 June 1968

Although the fight for Hue was over, much fighting remained to be done in the area to eliminate the large number of enemy units that had filtered in amongst the populated areas in the coastal lowland paddies, hedgerows and sand dunes surrounding the coastal village of Quang Dien, northeast of Hue. In the late spring these efforts were focused on a major counteroffensive conducted in Quang Tri and Thua Thien Provinces, which encompassed three major operations; 'Carentan', 'Carentan II/Lam Son 216', and 'Nevada Eagle' ('Lam Son 224').

In advance of the counteroffensive, it was decided to move the division to I Corps. Division headquarters and support battalions were airlifted north in late February and March; the division base camp (Camp Eagle) was established on 8 March off Highway 1 north of Phu Bai.

Operation 'Carentan'
8 March–31 March 1968

That same day Operation 'Carentan I' – named for the Normandy victory of June 1944 – was launched with 3rd Brigade of the 82nd Airborne Division on secondment. The initial assault was led by elements of 82nd Airborne, together with members of B Troop, 2nd Squadron (Airborne), 17th Cavalry Division and F Company, 58th Infantry Long-Range Reconnaissance Patrol (LRRP).

On 10 March, in a pattern that would be repeated on an almost daily basis over the coming two weeks, large weapons caches and rice stocks were uncovered. While clearing the area 501st and 502nd Infantry engaged regular and irregular forces north of Hue, along Route 547 leading out of Hue toward Fire Support Base (FSB) Bastogne. On 21 March, late in the evening, the North Vietnamese made a daring attack on the night defensive perimeter of the 2nd Battalion, 501st Infantry, using B-40 rockets as covering fire. Responding with small arms, automatic weapons and direct artillery fire, the paratroopers drove the enemy force off, killing 22. The following day, five miles west of Hue, gunships of B Company, 101st Aviation Battalion, caught a company of NVA in an open field, killing 34. Later three sampans were destroyed by a light fire team (LFT) from the battalion, resulting in nine more enemy deaths. Sweeping north of Hue, the 1st Battalion, 501st Infantry, met with stiff enemy resistance, indicating a sizeable force in

Below: Lt Steven Page of the 326th Engineer Battalion supervises the positioning of fuel bladders by an M578 Vehicle Tracked Recovery at Fire Support Base Bastogne on 16 April 1968. Fuel was the lifeblood of the airmobile divisions and their fleets of helicopters consumed it in vast quantities.

the area, later discovered to be the 803rd PAVN Regiment. A 48-hour battle ensued, in which more than 50 enemy were killed and more weapons recovered.

31 March – the last day of Operation 'Carentan' – saw no let-up in the relentless search for enemy soldiers and Viet Cong around Hue. Fifteen miles northwest of the city, the 1st Battalion (Airborne), 321st Artillery, trapped 85–100 NVA soldiers in an open field with accurate fire. Thirty of the NVA were killed. Six and a half miles west of Hue, members of the 1st Battalion (Airborne) 501st Infantry encountered a well-positioned enemy company. Air strikes were called in, resulting in 18 more enemy dead.

For the statisticians in Washington the operation was a great success. 861 enemy were killed. The total weapons and munitions captured included 186 individual and crew-served weapons, along with 1,027 rocket, mortar and artillery rounds. More than 41,000 rounds of small arms ammunition and 45 hand grenades were captured, along with nearly 17 tons of rice and grain.

On 5 April, Operation 'Pegasus/Lam Son 207' finally relieved Khe Sanh and thereby opened Route 9 for the first time since August 1967. This operation not only severely restricted PAVN movements in western Quang Tri Province but also inflicted casualties on the remnants of two North Vietnamese divisions withdrawing from the area. Preparations were by this time already underway at 1st Cavalry HQ for a major strike into the A Shau valley.

'Carentan II/Lam Son 216'
1 April–17 May 1968, Quang Tri Province, I Corps, South Vietnam

On the first day of April, with 'Carentan' only recently concluded, the 1st and 2nd Brigades, together with the 3rd Brigade, 82nd Airborne Division, launched Operation 'Carantan II', a continuation of Operation 'Carentan' in the same area of operations.

On 5 April a platoon of NVA was spotted in an open field north of Hue by a forward observation post of the 1st Battalion, 501st Infantry, and blasted by the guns of the 1st Battalion, 321st Artillery. Twenty-two enemy soldiers were killed. The same day, C Company of the 1st Battalion, 501st Infantry, engaged the enemy in two successful ambush attempts and fought a two-hour battle north of Hue that resulted in 21 enemy killed.

On 6 April, at a village 10 miles southwest of Hue, members of A Company, 2nd Battalion, 502nd Infantry, engaged a PAVN company in a network of bunkers. After the supporting barrage was lifted, paratroopers from the 1st Brigade's B Company, 2nd Battalion, 502nd Infantry, moved in to ring the village with a night perimeter. An attempt to break through the small cordon proved unsuccessful and resulted in two enemy killed. At first light, A Company paratroopers swept

Below: A soldier from Company A, 326th Engineer Battalion (Airborne) uses his AN/PRS 3 metallic mine detector to search for enemy weapons or booby traps in a pile of rice stalks.

through the village, uncovering 27 NVA bodies, and capturing six weapons. That same day, members of B Company, 1st Battalion, 501st Infantry, claimed 27 enemy kills and captured eight weapons in a battle 10 miles southwest of Hue. In another action, riflemen from A Company, 2nd Battalion, 501st Infantry, accounted for 17 dead PAVN 35 miles northwest of Hue.

Between 11 and 13 April A, B and D Companies of 2nd Battalion, 501st Infantry, cordoned A Phong Dien, a village 10 miles northeast of Hue along the 'Street Without Joy', which had been occupied by PAVN. A sweep of the village following a night of constant bombardment found 66 enemy dead and 26 weapons. Meanwhile paratroopers of A and C Companies, 1st Battalion, 501st Infantry, and A, B and C Companies of the 82nd Airborne's 1st Battalion, 505th Infantry, ended a week-long search and destroy mission along the Song Bo, three miles northwest of Hue. Army aviation, artillery, tactical air and the airborne troopers combined to kill 200 enemy and capture 44 weapons.

Eighteen miles north of Hue, elements from the 2nd Battalion, 501st Infantry discovered an enemy base camp on 16 April containing 20 underground tunnels and bunkers. Stored in the tunnels were 1,000 AK-47 rounds, 20 rounds for 60 mm mortars and various medical supplies. In the 1st Brigade AO, A and B Companies, 2nd Battalion, 327th Infantry, killed 12 NVA and captured five weapons during a fierce battle 12 miles southwest of Hue.

The following day, 17 April, a battalion-size cordon was established by paratroopers of the 1st Battalion, 501st Infantry, at the fortified village of Dong Xuyen three miles north of Hue. Following Army aviation, artillery and tactical air strikes, the troopers entered the village, and in three days had accounted for 53 enemy dead. Eight more kills were recorded by B Company, 2nd Battalion, 327th Infantry.

Above: As an airmobile division, the 101st was supported by considerable aviation assets that came under the 101st Aviation Group, formerly the 160th Aviation Group. The latter was formed on 1 July 1968 to convert the 101st Airborne Division to its new airmobile configuration. It was redesignated as the 101st Aviation Group on 25 June 1969 and comprised the 101st, 158th and 159th Aviation Battalions, the 163rd Aviation Company (General Support) and the 478th Aviation Company (Heavy Helicopter) as well as the 2nd Squadron, 17th Cavalry (Air) in the divisional reconnaissance role.

Casualties for both operations were US 193 KIA, 1,190 WIA, 11 MIA; enemy 1,892 KIA and 69 POWs.

The A Shau Valley: Operation 'Delaware'
19 April–17 May 1968

At this point, mid-way through 'Carentan II', the 1st Brigade of 101st Airborne Division was seconded to the 1st Air Cavalry. During the following month, together with elements of the 196th Infantry Brigade of ARVN 1st Division and an ARVN airborne task force, it undertook the first strike in two years into the A Shau Valley: Operation 'Delaware/Lam Son 216'. Though tentative plans had been made for a singular allied spoiling operation against this enemy redoubt sometime before, final preparations were only concluded in the last days of Operation 'Pegasus'. The 1st Brigade of 101st Airborne committed three infantry battalions; 196th Infantry Brigade committed three more and 1st Cavalry Division committed seven infantry battalions plus the 1st, 9th Cavalry.

The A Shau Valley

The A Shau Valley runs 35 miles along the Vietnam–Laos border, between two high mountain ranges. Its tactical value as a main supply and infiltration route from Laos into Thua Thien and Quang Nam Provinces rendered it an area of contest for many years. In late April 1968 it was the target of one of the 101st's toughest missions.

Not least of the problems was the terrain, for the thickly-wooded mountains flanking the sides of the valley climb to over 3,000 feet with the angle of slope varying from 20–45°. Also, the Laotian border is barely six miles away, and at that time within easy access of PAVN/VC safe havens and logistical bases. The North Vietnamese forces had been in control of the valley since March 1966 when they overran the Special Forces camp at the southern end. Since that time they had built a major base for the infiltration of personnel and supplies from North Vietnam through Laos along Route 547 into Thua Thien Province and the northern I Corps Tactical Zone. Furthermore, the PAVN had concentrated a very large amount of its anti-aircraft resources in the valley, meaning that the pilots flying into it would face what was undoubtedly the heaviest and most sophisticated enemy air defence encountered in airmobile operations up to that time.

Operation 'Delaware' envisaged a move through the valley to pre-empt enemy preparations for an attack on the Hue area, block off their communication routes leading out of the A Shau valley toward Hue, and take advantage of the damage done to the enemy by 'Pegasus'.

This was to be achieved by a coordinated airmobile and ground attack on two axes, using elements of three divisions: the 1st Cavalry, 101st Airborne and 1st ARVN Division. The 1st Cavalry, forming the initial prong, was to assault into A Luoi and Ta Bat on the valley floor. The 101st Airborne Division's role, in coordination with the 3rd ARVN Airborne Task Force, was to complement the 1st Cavalry assault by attacking along and astride Routes 547 and 547A, and interdict the enemy's routes of withdrawal and infiltration in the area. The 101st Airborne's FSB Bastogne, far to the east on Route 547, would just be able to reach the north end of the A Shau Valley with its long range 175-mm guns. The ARVN Airborne Task Force was to be responsible for clearing Route 547A.

During the period 14–19 April, over 100 B-52 sorties, 200 Air Force and Marine fighter sorties, and numerous aerial rocket artillery missions were ordered by the commander of the 1st Cavalry Division to identify and neutralise the AA sites concentrated in the valley. Also at this time, the 1st Brigade, 101st Airborne, and the ARVN Airborne Task Force were moved into pre-assault positions ready to make a separate attack on D-day east of the A Shau. Two major fire support bases were built up:

Below: Lt Robert Birch of Company A, 2nd Battalion, 501st Infantry (Airmobile), 2nd Brigade, 101st Airborne fills his one-quart plastic canteen with water from two-gallon cylinders on Hill 549 some 15km southwest of Hue on 28 January 1969. Such vital water containers were readily carried by resupply helicopters or as an underslung load.

the 47-day operational period the combined force had killed 2,100 PAVN troops, captured 157 prisoners and 581 weapons. Most importantly, it had to a large extent fulfilled the mission goal of relieving the pressure on the area around Hue.

Operation 'Nevada Eagle'

Also on 17 May, Operation 'Nevada Eagle', the most protracted of all the operations to which the 101st Airborne was committed, was initiated by the 1st and 2nd Brigades and the 3rd Brigade of the 82nd Airborne Division in Thua Thien Province, in the I Corps AO. The operation, which ran for 288 days from May 1968 to February 1969, was designed to deny the enemy the rice crop soon to be harvested in the lowlands of Thua Thien. Its larger purpose was to drive the enemy out of the plains and into the mountains where they could be tracked down and destroyed. During the operation allied forces carried out numerous sweeps through the valley, but there were few contacts of any size. Those of note are detailed below.

The first real contact occurred on 20 May when, exploiting intelligence information, members of B Company, 1st Battalion, 501st Infantry, trapped an enemy force in Dong Gi Tay village northeast of Hue. Three more rifle companies and one Popular Forces (PF) platoon were rushed in to cordon the village, and heavy casualties were inflicted on the enemy. A second minor action was touched off when airborne infantrymen from A Company, 2nd Battalion, 327th Infantry, were subjected to a mortar attack and an attempt to infiltrate their night defensive perimeter. The enemy was driven off with artillery and small arms fire, and a sweep of the area the next morning revealed 31 dead.

The only major action of 'Nevada Eagle' was fought on the night of on 21–22 May. Just after midnight, while most of the division was engaged on sweeps along the mountains in Thua Thien, a PAVN battalion, augmented by personnel from a sapper demolition team, launched a daring ground attack against Camp Eagle. Following a

Below: Marked by a purple smoke grenade, a UH-1D Command and Control helicopter carrying the brigade commander comes into land at the command post of the 2nd Battalion, 502nd Infantry (Airborne), 1st Brigade, 101st Airborne Division (Separate) during Operation 'Cook' in the mountains of Quang Ngai Province on 6 September 1967.

preparatory barrage in which more than 400 rounds of 122 mm rockets, 82 mm mortars, B-40 and B-41 ammunition were targeted on the division headquarters area, sappers attacked the 1st Brigade's positions at Gia Le on the southwest edge of the perimeter.

One 10-man sapper team managed to penetrate through the barbed wire as far as the brigade helipad, nearly half a mile inside the perimeter, before being chased off by a lone trooper. The attack was finally beaten back by the 1st Brigade's H&HC troops, members of the 2nd Battalion, 502nd Infantry, and swarms of helicopter gunships. Fast-thinking gunners from the 320th Artillery rolled in a 105 mm howitzer without sighting devices and killed 12 enemy at the edge of the wire with four 'Beehive' anti-personnel rounds.

At first dawn, a sweep of the area revealed 54 enemy bodies and 16 individual weapons. Additional ordinance uncovered included 40 satchel charges, 30 bangalore torpedoes, and 50 RPG rounds. Damage to the base area was minimal, but the action proved that the enemy had lost none of their audacity and daring.

In the following days, 327th Infantry units sweeping the mountains of Thua Thien made some spectacular discoveries. North of FSB Veghel, the 1st Battalion captured three light artillery pieces, two anti-aircraft guns and one truck, together with 23 mm and 85 mm ammunition and fuses. Yet better was to come. The largest haul of 'Nevada Eagle' was uncovered by members of A Company, 2nd Battalion along Route 547, 12 miles southwest of Hue nestled in the triple canopy jungle. Hidden in several 5 by 8 ft bunkers under three feet of overhead cover they found a cache of 238 individual and crew-served enemy weapons. The cache included 167 SKS rifles and 32 cases of new AK-47s. The same unit found a second major arms cache in a bunkered enemy base camp four miles east of the A Shau valley, this one containing 12 complete 60 mm mortars, 150 bolt-action Chicom rifles (K-44), four light machine guns, 80 rifle grenades and 40 B-40 rockets. And at the end of the month 49 enemy trucks and four 23 mm anti-aircraft guns with 2,100 rounds of ammunition were captured along a road 15 miles southwest of Hue by elements of the 1st Battalion. The trucks were intact but minus their engines; closer investigation of the scene unearthed the missing engines buried 5–10 yards alongside them!

A third major discovery was made on 29 May, by riflemen from A Company, 2nd Battalion. The haul included 107 SKS rifles, 59 K-44 rifles, four AK-47s, 102 rounds of 75 mm shells, 5,660 rounds of small arms ammunition, 3,300 grenade fuses, 26 B-41 rockets and 24 rounds of 60 mm mortar ammunition. Rounding out actions in May, a two-day cordon operation seven miles east of Hue near Le Xa Dong hamlet was conducted by B Company, 1st Battalion, 501st Infantry, with the 2nd Squadron of the 17th Cavalry and elements of the 1st ARVN Division. Some 91 PAVN were killed, 19 prisoners taken and 34 weapons captured.

On 3 June another major weapons cache was seized by A Company, 2nd Battalion, 327th Infantry, in the coastal plains area. The same day marked the end of a two-day cordon around Trung Phuong hamlet, three miles southeast of Hue, where a multi-company airborne task force composed of 17th Cavalry, the 2nd Brigade of the 101st Airborne and ARVN airborne troopers killed 66 enemy, took 51 prisoners and captured 55 weapons. On the fourth, paratroopers of A Company, 2nd Battalion, 327th Infantry, continued to uncover large quantities of weapons as they conducted an extensive search of the complex found on 3 June. Added to the previous total were 87 AK-47s, 174 AK-47 magazines with 1,500 rounds of ammunition, and more than 300 82 mm mortar rounds.

From early June the rice denial programme also began to yield some spectacular successes. In the first two weeks of the month, allied forces seized rice in large quantities from caches scattered throughout the 'Nevada Eagle' AO. Added to the weight of rice already captured, the haul now amounted to more than 156 tons, all of which was distributed to various district chiefs throughout Thua Thien province.

Above: SP4 David Weeks of Company L, 75th (Ranger) Infantry, 101st Airborne Division (Airmobile), sets up an M18A1 Claymore mine as part of a training exercise at the MACV Recondo School, operated by the 5th Special Forces Group (Airborne), 1st Special Forces, on Hon Tre Island in the Bay of Nha Trang, one of the most beautiful areas of South Vietnam and a Special Forces adventure playground throughout the war. The Claymore Anti-Personnel Mine was a fearsome weapon that spewed out 700 steel balls with a killing range of 50m and was fired either by a trip wire or a hand-held initiator.

And this is the way it went on, week after week. Two months into the operation, more than 1,100 of the enemy had been killed, 235 taken prisoner, nearly 2,000 weapons taken, and the rice haul stood at 280 tons. However, Communist units had thus far refused to be drawn into major conflict and successfully used mines and booby traps to inflict US casualties. 'Nevada Eagle' also revealed the North Vietnamese ability to entice US helicopter pilots into ambushes by using small groups as bait and then, as the helicopters came in to engage, opening fire with concealed weapons.

Other operations

In III Corps area during the period 5–12 May 1968, the Viet Cong launched an offensive with Saigon as the primary objective. Small Viet Cong cells did manage to get into the outskirts but these were easily fragmented and driven out, and at no point was the city in danger of being overrun as had nearly been the case in January.

COUNTEROFFENSIVE, PHASE V

1 July–1 November 1968

Beginning in the summer of 1968 a countrywide effort was begun to restore government control of territory lost to the enemy since the Tet offensive. The enemy attempted another such offensive on 17–18 August, but again their efforts were comparatively disjointed and were quickly overwhelmed by Allied forces. In the autumn the South Vietnamese government, with major US support, launched an accelerated pacification campaign. All friendly forces were coordinated and brought to bear on the enemy in every tactical area of operation. In these intensified operations, friendly units first secured a target area, and then Vietnamese government units, regional/popular forces, police and civil authorities screened the inhabitants, seeking members of the Viet Cong infrastructure. This technique was deemed so successful against the communist political apparatus that it became the basis for subsequent friendly operations. Government influence expanded into areas of the countryside previously dominated by the Viet Cong to such an extent that two years later at least some measure of government control was evident in all but a few remote regions.

Above: Two 'redlegs' of the 2nd Battalion, 320th Artillery (105mm) (Airborne), 1st Brigade, 101st Airborne Division (Separate), plot a fire mission for their 105mm howitzers at Fire Support Base Berchtesgaden during August 1968. The standard towed 105mm howitzer was the fundamental artillery weapon of the Vietnam war and provided the majority of the fire support to the infantry operating in the hostile countryside. However the limited HE charge of the 105mm shell was often ineffective in the dense jungles of Vietnam.

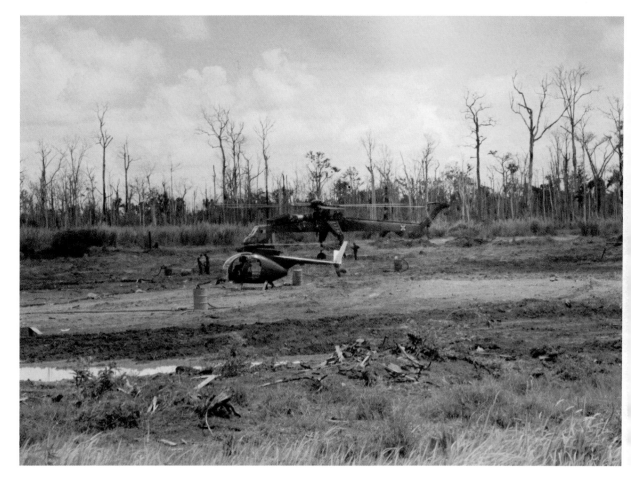

Above: A CH-54A Tarhe towers over a diminutive OH6A Cayuse at a refueling point in the field. US Army helicopters were named after native American tribes such as the UH-1 Iroquois but most acquired unofficial nicknames. The Tarhe was commonly known as the 'Skycrane' or 'Flying Crane' as that was on of its principal roles. The markings on the tail boom of this Skycrane indicate the 478th Aviation Company (Heavy Helicopter). With the callsign Hurricane, the four Skycranes were attached to the 159th Aviation Battalion (Assault Support Helicopter) as the heavy lift capability the 101st Airborne Division (Airmobile) in the latter years of the war.

The second airmobile division

On 28 June 1968 US Army, Pacific, published General Order 325, which initiated reorganisation of the 101st Airborne Division into the Army's second airmobile division. This order called for the division to be redesignated the 101st Air Cavalry Division, effective 1 July 1968. However, the term 'air cavalry division' was revoked by the Department of the Army on 26 August 1968, and the designation was re-established as the 101st Airborne Division (Airmobile).

Conversion of the 101st to an airmobile configuration had been considered by the Department of the Army prior to the deployment of the 2nd and 3rd Brigades in December 1967. However, the continued deficit in aviation assets during the build-up of forces in Vietnam had made such conversion impractical. The division developed a three-phase plan to accomplish the conversion from the airborne to the airmobile configuration, under which it would swap its 15,000 or so parachutes for more than 400 helicopters.

The first phase (1 July to 1 December 1968) would involve the activation and organisation of the 160th Aviation Group and a reorganisation of the division base. The second phase, which would not be completed until June 1969, involved the conversion of the armoured cavalry squadron to an air cavalry squadron. The last phase involved the activation of an aerial rocket artillery battalion. It was predicted that the whole process would take a full year, given the need to procure aviation assets and the fact that the division would continue to conduct combat operations throughout the conversion period. As it turned out, the reorganisation progressed smoothly with a few exceptions, one of these being in the aircraft maintenance area.

On 19 July 1968, command of the 101st Airborne Division officially passed from Major General O.M. Barsanti, to Major General Melvin Zais. During his seven months in the field, Barsanti had won the respect of his men with a lead-from-the-front approach, for which he received the Distinguished Service Cross, two Silver Stars and five Purple Hearts.

Back to the A Shau: Operation 'Somerset Plain'

In August 1968, the 101st Airborne began preparing for a move back into the A Shau, where a task force composed of units of 101st Airborne, 3rd Brigade of 82nd Airborne and ARVN 1st Infantry was to conduct a search-and-destroy operation to clear the enemy from the valley and attempt to bring them to a decisive battle – something the MACV had long craved.

Operation 'Somerset Plain' started on 3 August with the 2nd Battalion, 502nd Infantry, and the 2nd Battalion, 327th Infantry, combat-assaulting the valley floor near the old A Luoi and Tabat airstrips. The assault did not go well. One F-4 fighter-bomber and no less than 17 helicopters were felled by the intense anti-aircraft fire. Two battalions of the ARVN 1st Division and the 1st Battalion, 327th Infantry, joined the battle later that day.

The main objective of the initial phase was to disrupt enemy movements that might lead to an assault toward the lowlands. However, once the landing zones had been secured and the ARVN and US units had linked up, the PAVN broke contact and began to move towards the safety of Laos. Things took another wrong turn when on 10 August, a F-100 Super Sabre accidentally strafed the 101st Airborne troops, killing seven and

Above: An M102 105mm howitzer of the 2nd Section, Battery C, 2nd Battalion, 320th (105mm) (Airborne), 1st Brigade, 101st Airborne, fires in support of ground troops during Operation 'Somerset Plain' in the A Shau Valley in August 1968. During the 17-day operation, 170 NVA were killed with four POWs and 58 weapons captured. The M102 had an effective range of 11,500m and a battery of six guns could saturate a target with 48 33lb HE shells in one minute. A well-drilled battery could have 36 rounds in the air before the first one landed.

wounding 54 others. The operation rapidly degenerated into a small series of patrolling actions, with no real contact with the enemy. Allied losses were 34 killed and 161 wounded; 171 PAVN were killed, four were taken prisoner and 58 weapons captured. Although claimed as a victory in the aftermath by MACV, which stated that the enemy 'had been driven out of the A Shau', this was clearly not true. All told, it would be difficult to label 'Somerset Plain' a success, although this should not be attributed to any fault in the performance of the 101st Airborne Division.

Meanwhile operations continued in Thua Thien Province under 'Nevada Eagle'. September saw a rather more successful sweep than that recently undertaken in the A Shau, in which 'classic' cordon tactics were utilised to trap and eliminate PAVN troop concentrations instead of trying to draw them into the kind of set-piece battles that they knew well to avoid.

In this operation, the 1st Battalion, 501st Infantry, participated in the 11-day combined-force cordon of Vinh Loc Island, a 15-mile-long peninsula lying in the South China Sea. The VC had moved in after the Tet Offensive, and had since used the district as a recuperation area and supply base. In the early morning of 11 September the 101st Airborne men, together with the 1st Battalion, ARVN 54th Regiment, air-assaulted to landing zones on the eastern coast while armoured personnel carriers of the 3rd Squadron, ARVN 7th Cavalry, moved in from the north. The US Navy's Swift Boats and the Hue River Security Group sealed off the island on the seaward side. During the following 11 days, the airborne troopers and ARVN soldiers made a systematic search of the southern half of the island, rounding up VC suspects. When the operation was over, 154 enemy had been killed, 178 weapons captured and 126 members of the VC infrastructure on the island captured. In addition, 53 enemy had rallied to the government.

In the late autumn 'Nevada Eagle' was focused inland of Thua Thien Province; the same pattern of sweeps in the mountains and continual ambushes and patrols in the coastal plains continued. Also in September 1968, the 3rd Brigade redeployed to I Corps at Phong Diem, just to the south of Quang Tri.

COUNTEROFFENSIVE, PHASE VI

2 November 1968–22 February 1969

By late 1968 the unshakeable confidence on which had been built the colossal United States military apparatus in Vietnam was showing signs of cracking. The unsatisfactory results in Vietnam, growing domestic opposition to the war and a changing international political climate were leading some of those in Washington to ask serious questions about America's future role in Vietnamese – and global – politics.

In the autumn of 1968, Richard M. Nixon was elected president, and concurrent with his taking office a change of policy was brought about. In January 1969 Nixon announced a coming end to US combat operations in Southeast Asia and a simultaneous strengthening of South Vietnam's ability to defend itself. Already, in November 1968, the South Vietnam government with American support had began a concentrated effort to expand security in the countryside, known as the 'Accelerated Pacification Campaign'. Perhaps most significant of all, formal truce negotiations began in Paris on 25 January 1969.

Away from the negotiating tables it was business as usual, with no less than 47 ground combat operations recorded during this period. Operation 'Nevada Eagle' was still proving successful in severely limiting enemy activity in Thua Thien Province, if not in bringing them to battle. The sweeps and rice collection programme continued to score results; From 7 May, when 'Nevada Eagle' started, to the beginning of December, 2,759 enemy were killed and 803 prisoners captured, along with enormous quantities of arms,

Left: A Huey mechanic grabs some much needed rest in a hammock improvised beneath the tail stinger of a UH-1H at Camp Evans. The many helicopters of the 101st Airborne Division (Airmobile) came under the control of the 101st Aviation Group – in the words of the divisional commander, Major General John M Wright – 'The 101st lived by helicopters. Other divisions had to ask for helicopter support but in the 101st the helicopters stayed in the field. We had over 400 helicopters organic to the division, able to react immediately to calls from commanders. We had the lift plus weapons helicopters for support. It just replaced the jeep. It was that common in the 101st.'

Below Left: Another day, another drop as a Huey comes into land on a resupply run for men of Company A, 2nd Battalion 501st Infantry (Airmobile), 1st Brigade, 101st Airborne Division (Airmobile), at Fire Support Base Birmingham located on Hill 549, some 15kms southwest of Hue on 28 January 1969. The majority of helicopter sorties in Vietnam were simple administrative 'ash and trash' runs such as this but the provision of fresh provisions and mail in the field was vital for troop morale.

Above: A gaggle of Huey 'slicks' of the 158th Aviation Battalion (Assault Helicopter) lands at Camp Evans on 30 May 1969 to pick up more supplies for the 3rd Brigade, 101st Airborne Division (Airmobile), during Operation 'Apache Snow' in the A Shau Valley following the battle of Hamburger Hill that proved to be a turning point of the division's operations in Vietnam.

ammunition, equipment and rice. A rather morbid statistic from this war of numbers is given in a routine report written early in the month. From this it was learned that the milestone of 10,000 enemy killed by the 101st was reached late in November.

During early December, activity in the AO was confined to some minor skirmishes. Of more interest is the two-phase action of 11–14 December, when the 1st Battalion, 501st Infantry, combined with ARVN troops, the Hue River Security Group and National Police, assaulted by air and sea to cordon the northern part of Vinh Loc Island. This was a reprise of the tactics that had earlier proved so successful. On the first day, 500 persons were screened, with five classified as VC.

14 December marked the start of the fourth in the series of combined forces operations around Phu Vang. The 1st Battalion of the 506th Infantry, and 3rd Battalion of the187th Infantry (with the ARVN 54th Regiment) conducted multi-battalion air assaults into landing zones near Fire Base (FB) Maureen, which then directed a major effort against a PAVN 6th Regiment base area near Phu Vang. The 1st Battalion, 501st Infantry, teamed with the 54th ARVN Regiment to conduct further cordon and search missions aimed at preventing PAVN and VC units from regrouping in the area east and southeast of Hue.

On Christmas Eve the traditional ceasefire was observed and was mostly peaceful. On Christmas Day however, at FB Anzio, Company C, 2nd Battalion, 502nd Infantry fought off an attack on their perimeter. Early the following day, the battalion's A Company fought a running battle with a platoon of enemy soldiers who were moving out of a nearby village.

As the year came to its close, the division initiated a year-round offensive, a combined forces operation in Nam Hoa District aimed at PAVN battalions in the area. It was initiated with multiple air assaults by the 1st Battalion of the 506th Infantry and ARVN troops along the Song Thao Ma. Elsewhere, elements of 3rd Battalion, 506th Infantry, in the southern part of II Corps area killed two VC in two contacts and captured large quantities of food and medical supplies.

TET 69/COUNTEROFFENSIVE

23 February 1969–8 June 1969

By late 1969, US forces operating within South Vietnam had radically changed their tactics. They began to base their operations on the heavily gunned 'fire-bases', from where they sent out sorties and launched sweeping manoeuvres into known enemy territory. With increased support from aircraft and artillery, infantry platoons or company-sized units would frequently set out to ambush, reconnoitre or destroy the enemy.

Although Tet 1969 was largely peaceful, soon after the three-day holiday through the month of June, PAVN/VC units again tried to sustain an offensive. These efforts were by and large thwarted by aggressive allied ground operations; in this period a total of 70 significant named ground operations were terminated country wide.

Operation 'Nevada Eagle' continued in the new year with the same objectives as before: to defeat enemy personnel in small-scale actions, and to capture rice caches, materiel and installations within its AO. As before, offensive sweeps were undertaken along Route 547 and around Song Bo. It was not until three weeks into the post-Tet offensive that the divisional HQ at Hue was attacked by some rockets, which caused little damage. This was cited by some as evidence that Thua Thien Province was largely pacified. At the end of February, Operation 'Nevada Eagle' ended. Over 4,000 PAVN/Viet Cong soldiers – the equivalent of eight 400-man battalions – had been killed, another two battalions captured, and yet two more had changed allegiance under the Chieu Hoi programme. At the same time enough weapons (3,702) were captured to arm nine enemy battalions. Perhaps most important of all, 668 tons of rice were taken – enough to feed the men of 10 battalions for about a year.

Impressive those these achievements were it should be pointed out that once again the main objective, to draw the enemy to a major battle, was never realised. Another familiar pattern was also repeated, in that that once the allied forces had left the valley, the PAVN/VC returned within a short time.

Operation 'Kentucky Jumper'
1 March–14 August 1969

On 1 March 1969, the 2nd Brigade initiated the first of three separate operations in Thua Thien Province that were known overall as 'Kentucky Jumper'. This was a division-wide effort over a 167-day period that encompassed Operations 'Massachusetts Striker', 'Apache Snow' and 'Montgomery Rendezvous'. In the words of the official operational report, the objectives were 'to interdict enemy base areas and infiltration routes, seek out and destroy PAVN/VC units, detect, capture or destroy local Viet Cong and their infrastructure and their sympathisers, and to disrupt the routes of supply between the rice producing lowlands and population centres, and mountain base areas'.

Unlike previous operations, Operations 'Massachusetts Striker' and 'Apache Snow' attempted to deny the enemy the use of the A Shau for an indefinite period of time, something that thus far had proven beyond the capabilities of US and ARVN forces. 'Striker' was directed against the southern portion of the valley, while 'Apache Snow' followed with the invasion of the northern area. Finally, 'Montgomery Rendezvous' aimed at clearing the eastern slope and the middle of the valley floor.

However, in contrast to their response to many previous operations, the PAVN resolved to stand its ground during Operation 'Kentucky Jumper', resulting in two particularly ferocious battles at 'Bloody Ridge' (Dong A Tay) and Dong Ap Bia – the infamous 'Hamburger Hill'.

Operation 'Massachusetts Striker'
A Shau Valley, 28 February–8 May 1969

Following closely in the wake of the latest withdrawal from the A Shau, MACV intelligence reported a predictable increase in PAVN logistical activity in the valley. Consequently, beginning on 1 March, the 101st Airborne went back to the valley for the third time under Operation 'Massachusetts Striker' to conduct further sweeps.

On the first day, A Company, 326th Engineering Battalion, was inserted onto a hilltop overlooking the valley. Under the protection of troopers of the 2nd Squadron, 17th Cavalry, they began construction of Fire Base Whip, the proposed forward base camp of the brigade.

From Whip the 2nd Brigade was to conduct operations in the southern A Shau and Rao Nai valleys, the success of which depended on bold insertions of the manoeuvre battalions, followed by forced combat marches to the Laotian border to cut off enemy withdrawals. Little intelligence was available regarding the enemy strength and disposition, but it was clear that they were highly trained, well-equipped, hard-core troops.

Almost as soon as the engineer company was on the ground, monsoon rains descended on the mountains. No flying was possible and the engineers had to continue their construction work without adequate food or water supplies. For days they subsisted on rainwater they could catch in their ponchos.

The bad weather persisted until finally, on 12 March, the 1st Battalion of the 502nd Infantry was able to stage forward as far as FB Veghel. However, unbeknown to them, a company of the PAVN 9th Regiment was dug in inside the perimeter of the abandoned position.

Above: An 81mm mortar crew of Company D, 1st Battalion, 501st Infantry (Airmobile), 2nd Brigade, 101st Airborne Division (Airmobile), disembarks from a UH-1H during an operation west of Tam Ky on 1 June 1969.

On the LZ, command-controlled mines had been emplaced and aimed skyward against incoming helicopters, and the area was heavily booby-trapped. Most of these defences were destroyed in an artillery preparation immediately before the assault.

When the assault helicopters carrying C Company swept down on Veghel at 1700 hrs, four of the first five choppers to land took hits although none were destroyed. Bitter fighting ensued as the clouds closed over again, cutting off air support.

By midnight, the enemy had stopped returning fire, and the following morning C Company's sweep of the area was completed with little difficulty. Twelve NVA bodies had been left inside the perimeter and eight more were found along the enemy's line of withdrawal.

That afternoon the rest of the battalion joined C Company at Veghel and began a drive westward toward the border in pursuit. For the next 33 days the battalion fought tooth and nail with the retreating enemy, pushing them back yard by yard, from one position to the next, until finally they made a stand at Dong A Tay, the battle of 'Bloody Ridge'. Throughout this period, for the first time, PAVN units exhibited unusual determination to stand and fight in the face of major losses rather than flee to sanctuaries in Laos.

Meanwhile on 20 March, 2nd Battalion, 501st Infantry, was inserted into the Rao Nai Valley, southeast of the A Shau, and from there pushed out toward the Laotian border. They encountered light resistance along the way from small delaying squad or platoon-size elements.

The final phase of the operation began two days later; the 'No Slack' Battalion of the 327th Infantry was transferred from the control of 1st Brigade to 2nd Brigade and invaded the old airstrip on the floor of the valley. This had originally been the destination of the 1st Battalion, 502nd Infantry, before it was committed to Dong A Tay. Again, little resistance was encountered as the troops moved quickly southward to the Laotian border on three axes. Delays caused by bad weather coupled with allied forces' activity on the edges of the valley had apparently telegraphed the approach of the battalion, and the enemy units withdrew into Laos before they could be overtaken.

Once both battalions had reached the border they retraced their steps and conducted intensive search operations in their respective areas. In the next several weeks enemy base camps, hospitals, high-speed trails and supply caches were discovered and destroyed or removed. The 'No Slack' paratroopers found several trucks and bulldozers along a heavy-duty road that PAVN engineers had been constructing and improving only days before. D Company, 2nd Battalion, 501st Infantry, came upon a way-station hospital complex and drove off what was apparently a caretaker platoon. That night, after the company established its night positions in the complex, the enemy platoon returned with satchel charges, RPG fire and small arms. The attack was repelled, three sappers dying inside the perimeter.

A few days later the 'Drive On' troopers, following a high-speed trail, found caches that contained 120,000 AK-47 rounds, dozens of rifles, rocket-propelled grenades and mortar rounds. They continued to be harassed by booby-traps and snipers and cache security guards.

By this time the 1st Battalion, 501st Infantry, had completed another successful cordon operation on the plains and joined 'Massachusetts Striker'. On 10 April they combat-assaulted into Fire Base Thor and the area southeast, spearheading the brigade's move into Quang Nam Province in the direction of Da Nang.

1st Battalion, 502nd Infantry, after mopping up operations at Dong A Tay, was inserted on 16 April into Fire Base Lash astride the so-called 'Yellow Brick Road' (Route 614), an important North Vietnamese supply route. Encountering virtually no resistance, C Company had soon unearthed a huge, 100-ton cache of electronic equipment and medical supplies. Further probes uncovered 14 trucks, over 600 brand-new SKS rifles, Chinese-built radios and field telephones, large stocks of medicine, large quantities of assorted supplies and equipment, and documents indicating the location of another cache.

As discoveries such as these continued, it became apparent that the entire area of the extreme southern A Shau had been abandoned by the PAVN, who had left the bulk of their equipment and munitions behind in their hasty retreat. Furthermore the 'Yellow Brick Road' was interdicted and destroyed by the 2nd Brigade, hampering enemy plans for future offensives against Hue and Da Nang.

When Operation 'Massachusetts Striker' ended on 8 May, the paratroopers had killed 176 enemy, and captured 859 individual and 34 crew-served weapons.

With rucksacks almost empty, the 2nd Brigade flew back to the coastal plains and almost immediately began preparing for the next operation.

At the beginning of April the 101st Airborne initiated Operation 'Texas Star' in western Quang Tri and Thua Thien Provinces. It was a joint operation in conjunction with the 1st ARVN Infantry Division, and the purpose was to regain the initiative in the mountains east of the A Shau Valley. This effort ran until 5 September 1970; fighting was heavy throughout the entire period, but the intensity steadily increased during late June and early July culminating with the battle for FSB Ripcord.

In mid-May the 1st Battalion, 501st Infantry, and the 'First Strike' battalion was deployed to the Tam Ky area to fight with the Americal.

Operation 'Apache Snow'
10 May–7 June 1969

While the 2nd Brigade were winding down their operations in the extreme southern portion of the A Shau, division staff were busy amending the plans to exploit a massive 'warehouse' area pinpointed by Cavalry units while making a B-52 strike assessment.

Codenamed 'Apache Snow', the operation was designed to destroy those enemy forces occupying the steep mountains rising abruptly from the A Shau Valley that separated I Corps from Laos. A combined allied force was to block their likely escape routes into Laos along Highway 922 and interdict Route 548. Running the length of the valley floor, this was currently being used as an infiltration route into the coastal lowlands of Thua Thien and Quang Nam Provinces. RIF operations would then find the enemy and their caches and destroy them.

Weeks before the jumping off day, in order to confuse the enemy and mask true intentions, more than 30 landing zones were 'prepped' by the Air Force. 10,000 lb 'daisy-cutter' bombs fused to detonate above the ground were dropped on these locations, clearing vegetation without making craters. Then, only 16 hours before the assault, artillery batteries were placed at FSBs Bradley, Airborne, Currahee, Berchtesgaden and Cannon.

With the preparations complete, Operation 'Apache Snow' was initiated at 0730 hrs on 10 May with the largest single airmobile assault of the Vietnam War. Some 65 UH-1 'Huey' helicopters transported seven battalions of the 101st Airborne, 1st ARVN Division and 9th Marine Regiment, 3rd Marine Division, from FSB Blaze to their start lines. The

Below: Troopers undergo in-country training at Dong Da Thien during April 1969 under the guidance of members of Detachment 51, 5th Special Forces Group (Airborne).

PRESIDENTIAL UNIT CITATION (ARMY), STREAMER EMBROIDERED DONG AP BIA MOUNTAIN

H&HC, 3d Brigade, 101st Airborne Division cited in Department of the Army General Orders 16, 31 March 1972 (along with other attached units):

During the period 10-21 May 1969 the foregoing assigned and attached units of the 3d Brigade, 101st Airborne Division distinguished themselves by extraordinary heroism in action against the enemy in the vicinity of Dong Ap Bia Mountain, A Shau Valley, Republic of Vietnam. The 3d Brigade commenced Operation 'Apache Snow' by striking at the enemy on his ground. For 4 days the enemy harassed the men of the Brigade with mortar rocket-propelled grenades, and small arms fire. Undaunted by this enemy action, the units of the 3d Brigade continued to uncover huge amounts of enemy stores and equipment and to destroy his forces. After pinpointing a stronghold on Dong Ap Bia Mountain, the Brigade launched a series of determined attacks during the ensuing 8 days to drive the well-trained-and-equipped enemy from his entrenched positions. Each day the enemy continued to infiltrate reinforcements to help repel the determined American and Vietnamese forces. After 8 days of intense combat, units of the Brigade broke through the enemy defenses and overran his bunker complexes. The battle continued for another 36 hours while the men of the Brigade searched for and destroyed all remaining pockets of enemy resistance. During the 12 days of battle the 3d Brigade and attached units eliminated more than 500 enemy troops; seized large quantities of weapons, explosives, and other military equipment; and captured tons of rice. The determination, devotion to duty, indomitable courage, and extraordinary heroism demonstrated by the members of the 3d Brigade, 101st Airborne Division and attached units are in keeping with the highest traditions of the military service and reflect great credit on them and the United States Army.

choppers crossed the valley in the south and then, using the terrain as a screen, turned north along the Laotian border and headed for the selected LZs. Aircraft had already bombed the LZs for 50 minutes, artillery followed with a 15-minute barrage, and finally came aerial rocket artillery helicopter attacks.

Covered by AH-1 Cobra gunships, the lead elements of the 3rd Battalion, 187th Infantry, and 1st Battalion, 506th Infantry, were inserted over a 45-minute period, with Companies B, C, and D and the command post of the 1st Battalion on the ground by 0815 hrs. Within minutes the soldiers were pushing from the west – to the enemy's complete surprise. It was a flawless combat assault and an outstanding example of the capabilities of an airmobile unit. For the succeeding three days 3rd Battalion, 187th Infantry, watched trails in the surrounding area for signs of activity, but with one very significant exception, there were few contacts.

The Battle of Dong Ap Bia: Hamburger Hill

On 11 May 1969, B Company troops were climbing a hillmass called Dong Ap Bia (Ap Bia Mountain or Hill 937), when suddenly they began receiving automatic weapons fire. Unseen on the crest, entrenched in tiers of fortified bunkers with well-prepared fields of fire, were the 7th and 8th Battalions of the 29th NVA Regiment.

Little did either side know that this same hill would become the scene of one of the most savage battles of the Vietnam War, a bloody meat-grinder of a battle at a place quickly dubbed Hamburger Hill.

Responding to the contact, the battalion commander manoeuvred his companies along ridges leading to the top of the hill to determine the strength of the enemy. Realising that he had stumbled across a significant force, the division commander ordered the 1st Battalion Currahee to reinforce the 187th Infantry on the hill that evening. But as they moved off, the men almost immediately came under heavy fire from enemy gunners, and precious little progress was made. Three paratroopers were killed and another 33 wounded.

The next day, friendly fire from two Cobra gunships killed two and wounded 35 others. For three days thereafter the combat situation remained static. The PAVN units sat tight in their hilltop bunkers while the 101st Airborne probed and looked for weaknesses, under cover of continual bombardment by artillery, aerial rocket artillery and air strikes.

On 14 May a combined assault by companies B, C and D of the 187th Infantry was thrown back with the loss of 12 men killed and 80 wounded. On 15 May Companies A and B tried another assault, but this too proved fruitless as the North Vietnamese and Viet Cong forces withstood all attempts to dislodge them and inflicted 36 additional casualties. Regrouping once more, Zais now brought up two additional battalions, 2nd/501st and 2nd/3rd ARVN, along with A Company of the 2nd Battalion, 506th Infantry.

With the encirclement of the hill complete, and with the ARVN battalions posted to seal off escape routes, on 18 May two full battalions – the 3rd Battalion of the 187th Infantry and 1st Battalion of the 506th Infantry – assaulted the enemy bunker complex for a second time in an effort to drive out the North Vietnamese troops. Delta Company was within 25 yards of the top when a monsoon struck, rapidly turning the slopes into an unscalable mudbath, and forcing the paratroopers to move off the hill again.

After nine days of battle, there had been nine unsuccessful attempts to take the hill. At 1000 hrs on the 20th another was launched, this time a simultaneous four-battalion assault from multiple directions. Moving cautiously up the hill once more, under the cover of intense artillery and air strikes that had already turned the slopes into a deathscape of shattered trees and shell holes, the paratroopers made a slow, tortuous climb, fighting hand to hand through the bunkers. By early afternoon they had at last overcome the remaining defenders and secured the crest. The airborne at last had their victory.

Thus was ended the battle for Hamburger Hill. Decimated, the PAVN 29th Regiment limped back over the border to Laos. For 10 days it had bravely withstood the avalanche of fire that had been dumped on the hill (over 500 tons of bombs and 70 tons of napalm) and had been shattered in the process. So too had 187th Infantry, which had to be completely rebuilt.

As their comrades crawled up the hill at Dong Ap Bia, B, C and D Companies of the 2nd Battalion, 506th Infantry, combat-assaulted into the warehouse area discovered prior to the start of 'Apache Snow'. Their mission, to locate and destroy an enemy command post (CP) complex thought to be in the area, and capture food and munitions caches, soon bore fruit. Within days C Company discovered both the CP complex and a field hospital. In addition, more than 10 tons of rice and 75,000 rounds of ammunition for individual and crew-served weapons were captured during the sweep.

'Apache Snow' was terminated on 7 June. In all, the month-long operation accounted for 675 enemy killed, three prisoners, 241 individual and crew-served weapons captured, and more than 100,000 rounds of ammunition discovered. Allied losses were 56 US dead and five South Vietnamese, almost all of them at Hamburger Hill. The price of victory for taking Hamburger Hill was and is a major bone of contention. Critics charge that it was ambiguous as well as overly costly; the hill itself had no strategic or tactical importance and was abandoned soon after its capture. Many say that the battle wasted American lives and exemplified the irrelevance of US tactics in Vietnam. One Senator labelled the assault 'senseless and irresponsible'.

Below: The Battle of Hamburger Hill.

Defending the operation, the commander of the 101st acknowledged that the hill's only significance was that the enemy occupied it. 'My mission,' he said, 'was to destroy enemy forces and installations. We found the enemy on Hill 937, and that is where we fought them.'

Whatever one's opinion, it was the beginning of the end for American involvement in Vietnam. Washington ordered MACV Commander General Creighton Abrams to avoid such encounters in the future, and to accelerate the pace of Vietnamisation. It led indirectly to the limiting of subsequent US military operations. 'Hamburger Hill' was the last major search and destroy mission by US troops during the war (and the last major engagement fought by the 101st Airborne). From this point forth small unit actions predominated.

Operation 'Texas Star': Hill 882

Although overshadowed by the actions at Dong Ap Bia, another significant action was fought during May under Operation 'Texas Star' on Hill 882 in the mountains west of FSB Veghel. Hill 882 lay in the Nam Hoa mountain range of Thua Thien province (northern I Corps Zone), running along the northeast side of the A Shau Valley. 2nd Battalion, 502nd Infantry, was inserted onto the hill with the primary mission of establishing new LZs in the area, but after landing, they were repeatedly ambushed by PAVN regulars and had to be withdrawn because of heavy casualties.

At this time FSB Ripcord was under construction in the Coc Muen mountain range, Nam Hoa district, as part of the 101st Airborne defence network in Thua Thien. Nearly 3,000 feet high, Ripcord was located close to North Vietnamese sanctuaries in Laos, and in dominant terrain along which enemy infiltration routes to the populated lowlands had to pass. Fully aware of the threat that FSB Ripcord represented to their movements, the enemy had already begun to concentrate their forces in the area in preparation for an attack.

Soon after the withdrawal of the 2nd Battalion of the 502nd Infantry, B Company, 1st Battalion of the 327th Infantry was sent in. Unbeknown to them, they were an advance party sent in as a blocking force for FSB Ripcord.

Army intelligence had warned the commander of a possible PAVN sapper-battalion base of operations in the area and he had ensured the men were carrying extra machine-gun barrels and ammunition. Also, each squad was carrying a 90 mm recoilless rifle. Unknown to the troops, the sapper unit was part of a full PAVN division, which was massing for a planned attack on FSB Ripcord. The CO, Captain Terry Mills, split the company into three platoons, sending two off the hill into the surrounding jungle and try to locate the enemy while using the other platoon for command and control and to adjust possible air strikes and other firepower that was available.

On the fourth day, a reconnaissance patrol ran into a PAVN ambush. Their scout dog was killed by three hits from RPG-7 (rocket-propelled grenade) fire. Moving further down the trail that night the squad set up a night defensive perimeter within 50 yards of the NVA sapper base camp. The next morning, a recce team began to explore the surrounding area, and at noon it too walked into an ambush. All except one man were disabled in the sudden fusillade of fire. Using the squad radio, he tried to call in artillery support, only to watch the rounds fall harmlessly hundreds of yards away.

By this time the main force was also under attack as the PAVN probed the area trying to pinpoint the company position. The reconnaissance team withdrew, and after regrouping set up a defensive perimeter. A 'dustoff' was called for the wounded, and the company began withdrawing to the top of Hill 882.

After being resupplied the next morning, B Company was ordered to assault the PAVN base camp. As they advanced slowly to contact, there was a brief but intense small-arms exchange, before the airborne troops pulled back over a small finger of the hill. From this relatively safe position they called in Cobra gunship attacks on the enemy base camp, followed by 105 mm and 155 mm artillery fire from surrounding fire bases.

In the early afternoon, Air Force jets began dropping 500 lb bombs, and once these had gone, then came the napalm. On the second run, one of the pilots miscalculated, spreading the blazing liquid all over the company position. Many men were horribly burned. But the napalm had also devastated the sapper camp and the airborne troops took it without a fight.

After the battle, the company moved off the hill and set up recons in the valley that led to FSB Cannon. At night, the troops could plainly make out red flashlights as the PAVN moved into position to attack FSB Ripcord.

Operation 'Lamar Plains'

For a three-month period from mid-May, the 1st Brigade of 101st Airborne was under the operational control of the Americal Division; from 15 May it was engaged in Operation 'Lamar Plains' in the Chu Lai/Tam Ky area south of Da Nang. The 1st Battalion, 502nd Infantry, made two significant discoveries in the mountains southwest of Tam Ky. On 1 July, it found a cache containing 111 individual weapons, 33 crew-served weapons, three tons of ammunition and 17 bicycles. The second find was a 15-building hospital complex. 'Lamar Plains' ended on 14 August, and the brigade was returned to control of the 101st Airborne.

Other operations

In central Quang Tri Province the 3rd Marine Division continued their long-running Operation 'Kentucky' in the Con Thien area of the demilitarised zone. Initiated on 1 November 1967, the operation was aimed at preventing enemy infiltration through the barrier, and was terminated on 28 February 1969.

At the same juncture Operation 'Scotland II', initiated on 15 April the previous year, was rounded out. This long-running, multi-battalion sweeper operation centred in and around Khe Sanh, and engaged two battalions of the 4th Marine Regiment.

The 9th US Infantry Division continued Operation 'Speedy Express', a IV-Corps-wide effort to interdict lines of enemy communication and deny the enemy the use of base areas. It was started on 1 December 1968 and terminated at the end of May 1969, and although engagements were typically small, the division did fight several sizeable actions.

Throughout the early part of January 1969, PAVN/VC units continued to avoid major contacts with the Allies. However, on 23 February US Navy units and installations at Da Nang, Tan An, Ben Luc, Go Dan Ha and Tra Cu came under attacks that suggested a new enemy offensive, but since many units in these areas were poised to meet these attacks they caused only minimal damage.

Below and Left: Troopers undergo in-country training at Dong Da Thien during April 1969 under the guidance of members of Detachment 51, 5th Special Forces Group (Airborne).

SUMMER–AUTUMN 1969

9 June–31 October 1969

During the summer and autumn of 1969, conduct of operations was increasingly turned over to the South Vietnamese, while US troops withdrew in greater numbers amid reaffirmations of support for the Republic of South Vietnam's government from the Nixon administration. Nixon himself announced the phased reduction of the US military presence in South Vietnam, which would be demonstrated initially by the withdrawal of 25,000 troops by 31 August 1969. In April 1969 American troop strength had peaked at 543,400; by mid-October this had dropped to 505,500.

Operation 'Montgomery Rendezvous'

Although enemy attacks now began to concentrate on South Vietnamese positions, as American units switched to small unit actions to avoid US combat deaths, there was still plenty of fighting for the 101st Airborne.

On 8 June, 'Montgomery Rendezvous', the third operation under the overall umbrella of 'Kentucky Jumper', jumped off in the familiar and feared terrain of the A Shau Valley. For the operation, the 3rd Brigade was once again teamed up with the 3rd ARVN Regiment. Their prime objective was to provide security for Engineer units constructing Route 547 into the valley, by seeking out PAVN forces in the high ground to the east.

The first objective for the engineers was to construct an airstrip on the valley floor near an abandoned French airstrip at Ta Bat. On the first day of the operation a company of infantry secured landing zones in the surrounding area, and a party of 326th Engineers was airlifted in. The following day CH-54 Tarhe 'Flying Cranes' and CH-46 Chinooks flew 48 sorties to bring in their heavy equipment. Drainage ditches were cut on either side of the strip, parts of the bog were filled in, trees were felled with explosives and cleared away. Fifty-four working hours later, the strip was complete, and ready to accept the first C-7A Caribou.

For several weeks previously, engineers of the 27th Engineer Battalion, 18th Engineer Brigade, had been slowly cutting their way from FB Birmingham through the jungle to create a graded road all the way from Camp Eagle to the A Shau. Most of the road, Route 547, was cut into the sides of steep, tree-lined hills.

The mountainous terrain made for some difficult going, but by 20 June the road was ready for use. A column of 80 tracked vehicles of the 3rd Squadron of the 5th Cavalry, 9th Infantry Division, 7th Cavalry and 1st ARVN Division left FB Blaze and Cannon early in the morning. The lead APCs reached the new Ta Bat airstrip seven hours later without incident.

While the support command troops toiled away in the valley floor, 3rd Brigade combat operations were focused on the eastern highlands. Generally, contact with the enemy was light, with the exception of spirited sapper attacks on FSB Berchtesgaden and Currahee on the mornings of 14 and 15 June, respectively. At FSB Berchtesgaden, sappers armed with satchel charges managed to penetrate through the perimeter wire; one even made it into the mess hall, only to be killed by a cook. Eighteen PAVN troops were found inside the wire after the attack was repelled, and 13 more in the immediate vicinity.

The 1st Battalion, 506th Infantry, repelled another sapper attack on Fire Base Berchtesgaden launched in the early morning hours of 24 August. Approximately 90 enemy sappers, supported by mortar crews on the surrounding ridgelines, attacked the base at approximately 0320 hrs and were stopped cold just a few feet from the nearest bunker by well-coordinated base defensive fire. Aided by Cobra helicopters from the 4th Battalion, 77th Aerial Rocket Artillery, the troopers killed 31 PAVN and captured 19 weapons.

Ten days previously, on 14 August, 'Montgomery Rendezvous' had ended, having succeeded in bringing much-needed armour support to the A Shau Valley. The results of the two-month operation were 390 enemy killed and 185 individual and 43 crew-served weapons captured. US losses were 87 dead.

The conclusion of 'Montgomery Rendezvous' also brought the curtain down on Operation 'Kentucky Jumper'. After 167 days of combat in and around the A Shau Valley, more than 1,550 enemy had been killed and 41 suspects detained, 1,612 individual weapons, and 185 crew-served weapons captured.

Below: An OH-6A 'Loach' of the 2nd Squadron, 17th Cavalry, flies 'nap of the Earth' to minimise enemy fire as it comes into land at Fire Base Victory on 16 October 1969. By late 1969, the firebase became the focus of divisional operations as the withdrawal of US forces accelerated. The division was now increasingly called upon to provide material support for ARVN formations.

Siege of FSB Ripcord

On 1 July 1970, the first enemy mortar rounds hit FSB Ripcord, ending a long period of anticipation for the men stationed at the isolated outpost. During the following three weeks they were subjected to intense artillery bombardment, and infantry attacks upon the perimeter. The battle reached a climax in the final week when a patrol ran into an enemy formation and lost 12 men and 50 wounded. Then, after a Chinook helicopter carrying a load of fuel took hits from a PAVN 12.5 mm anti-aircraft gun and crashed into Ripcord's ammo dump, exploding on contact, the decision was made to withdraw.

While supporting the extraction, the 101st Aviation Group was constantly exposed to heavy anti-aircraft and mortar fire from approximately 2,500 enemy troops of the 803rd and 6th PAVN Regiments. During the withdrawal, the commanding officer and two troopers were killed. All told, the 101st's losses were 61 killed and another 345 wounded.

For their bravery the 101st Aviation Group and its assigned units earned for themselves a Valorous Unit Award. In the words of the citation:

"Demonstrating aggressive determination and uncommon valour, the members of the 101st Aviation Group (Combat) (Airmobile), 101st Airborne Division (Airmobile) dauntlessly conducted the tactical redeployment of personnel and equipment from besieged FSB Ripcord. As a result of their unfailing tenacity and heroism in the face of massive enemy bombardment, the lives of numerous Americans were saved."

Quang Tri

In early autumn, plans were made for the redeployment of the 3rd Marine Division and on 30 September, the 1st and 2nd Battalions, 506th Infantry, were airlifted to Quang Tri Province to form a security screen for the move. Under the plan two airmobile battalions, supported by artillery FBs, were to be inserted along a line from the DMZ to just north of Khe Sanh in the southern portion of the province. These battalions would stop enemy movements from Laos and North Vietnam that could potentially interfere with the redeployment. On 2 October, the operation began when eight companies air-assaulted into two primary areas just south of the DMZ. First in was C Company, 1st Battalion, 506th Infantry, which was tasked with securing the area to be used as a battalion command post. All the others were landed without difficulty. Over the course of the next month, 3rd Brigade troopers stifled enemy attempts to disrupt the redeployment, encountering scattered contact with PAVN units, the bulk of which had already withdrawn to sanctuaries to the north and the west. On 8 November, as the Marines successfully completed their move, 3rd Brigade units closed down the northern AO. During the operation, a total of 59 enemy soldiers were killed and 22 individual and two crew-served weapons were captured.

By this time US operations had begun to take on a slightly different character, as efforts to Vietnamise the war gathered pace. Countrywide, the US Army initiated training programmes that aimed at raising the combat proficiency of South Vietnamese forces, and to allow them to assume greater responsibility for operations.

A relevant example of this is the pacification programme Operation 'Saturate', carried out by the 1st Battalion, 327th Infantry, in Phu Thu District of Thua Thien Province, from 5 October. Concurrent with the effort to Vietnamise the war, the battalion initiated a training programme for Regional Force companies in the district. It also organised a programme of medical care, with the emphasis on using Vietnamese nurses and doctors along with US personnel. Both of these were attempts to undermine the VC infrastructure known to be operating within Phu Thu, and damage its public credibility.

During the entire civic action and training programme, the hunt for the enemy went on as usual, but there were few contacts of any significance. However, the battalion sweeps did net dividends, as a significant number of enemy bunkers and booby traps were discovered and destroyed.

Below: Members of Company D, 1st Battalion, 502nd Infantry (Airmobile), 2nd Brigade, 101st Airborne Division (Airmobile) assault over the ridgeline of a hill during Operation 'Lamar Plain'. This operation was conducted by the division in conjunction with the Americal Division in Quang Tri Province between 16 May and 13 August 1969 and it resulted in 524 enemy casualties. Note (bottom) M79 grenade launcher. Known variously as the 'blooper' or 'thumper', the M79 40mm grenade launcher was a highly effective squad weapon.

Above: Members of Company E, 2nd Battalion, 501st Infantry (Airmobile), 2nd Brigade, 101st Airborne Division (Airmobile), service their quad .50-caliber M55 machine guns on 25 February 1970. These weapons proved fearsomely effective for the perimeter defence of fire support bases and other fixed installations. By this time dress regulations were increasingly lax and the boonie hat was the preferred choice of headgear.

WINTER–SPRING 1970

1 November 1969–30 April 1970

During this period, US and allied forces concentrated on operations to support the pacification programme. Particular effort was made in Vietnamisation through training and equipping RVN armed forces. Over the next few years, the ARVN was to be boosted to over 500,000 men. In turn this provided Nixon's administration with the necessary political means to recall three brigades of the US 1st Infantry Division and several major USMC units from Vietnam. At the end of 1969, America's fighting strength in Vietnam stood at 475,000; by the end of 1970 this had been reduced to 334,600.

During November a marked increase in enemy-initiated attacks signalled the start of the first phase of the Communist winter campaign. This was highlighted by intensified harassment incidents and attacks throughout the south. In November–December these were heaviest around Saigon, in III and IV CTZs, and were primarily directed against Vietnamese military installations in a clear attempt to disrupt the pacification programme. November was also marked by major attacks upon By Prang and Duc Lap in CTZ II (Central Vietnam).

By February 1970 the enemy had shifted their focus to I and II Corps. In the spring, attacks increased steadily, reaching a peak in April. Several efforts were made to take the offensive in the Central Highlands near I Corps CIDG camps at Dak Seang, Dak Pek and Ben Het. Dak Seang was attacked on 1 April 1970 and remained under siege throughout the month, until relieved by ARVN forces acting independently.

There were also numerous attacks by fire and several sapper attacks against US FSBs in I Corps through April and May.

In mid-November the 2nd Battalion, 501st Infantry, had just begun what was supposed to be a five-day stand-down at LZ Sally when it was ordered to deploy quickly to Quang Tri Province to assist elements of the 1st Brigade of the 5th Infantry Division. Many of the soldiers were being issued new clothing and cleaning their weapons and equipment when they were suddenly alerted for the move.

The eagerly anticipated opportunity to rest and relax rapidly was about to be rudely displaced by five days of heavy contact with the 27th PAVN Regiment in desolate hill country 20 miles west of Quang Tri. Within two hours of the alert, 18 CH-47 Chinooks were en route to Quang Tri Combat Base, with a 500-man force on board. There, over 40 UH-1 'slicks' took over the airlift and combat-assaulted their passengers into the area, where elements of the 1st Brigade, 5th Infantry, had been embroiled in fighting for several days.

In one notable action, B Company assaulted a large bunker complex only to become bogged down in a tit-for-tat firefight with the defenders. Under the eerie glow of flares and strobe lights, C Company launched a daring night manoeuvre to surround the fortified position. With Cobra gunships providing support, the airborne troops stormed the position, killing 29 PAVN troops.

Elsewhere, in a major series of engagements beginning on 28 January, 3rd Battalion, 506th Infantry, at that time OPCON to 173rd Airborne Brigade, battled the 8th Battalion of the 22nd PAVN Regiment in the area northwest of Bong Son, Binh Dinh Province, in northern II Corps area.

The firefights were initiated by PAVN troops hunkered down in the caves and crevices on Hill 474. Calling up air strikes by F-4 fighter-bombers and a massive artillery bombardment, battalion troops manoeuvred by helicopter to block potential escape and then systematically cleared the enemy positions. The PAVN lost 90 dead as a result, in addition to 23 weapons and thousands of rounds of ammunition captured.

Operation 'Randolph Glen'

The launch of Operation 'Randolph Glen' on 7 December marked the start of a clear departure from the more conventional use of combat forces in South Vietnam. On the edge of populated lowlands in eastern Thua Thien Province, 2nd Brigade of the 101st Airborne and ARVN units staged a series of Civil Action programmes under which they provided technical assistance to government officials. These were accompanied by coordinated, limited military actions and ran until 31 March 1970.

The 'Street Without Joy'

In mid-February, the 101st Airborne troops were called on to help in another such programme – the resettlement of the infamous 'Street Without Joy' in Phong Dien District. In the early 1950s, this 20-mile-long strip of sandy flatland north of Hue was ravaged by fierce battles between the French and the Viet Minh. During Tet, the PAVN advance forced the inhabitants to evacuate their homes, and for two years they were housed in government refugee camps.

By early 1969, the area had been largely cleared of enemy troops and the 101st Airborne was able to begin a massive effort to resettle the refugees in their former homes. The 3rd/187th was ordered to the area in October of 1969 to eradicate the remaining VC infrastructure and began the arduous task of clearing mines and booby traps. Shortly thereafter, engineers from the 326th Engineer Battalion started repair work on the roads. By late April, more than 8,000 people had returned to their homes.

The Cambodian Incursion

In early 1970, Nixon directed that PAVN sanctuaries, staging areas, and storage depots in the strip of Cambodia bordering South Vietnam be eliminated. For years this area had provided a haven for enemy activities, and it was considered an intolerable threat to the US policy of Vietnamisation.

May Day, the traditional Communist holiday, was marked in 1970 by the massed assault of a combined Allied force of 15,000 US and ARVN soldiers across the southern border of Vietnam aimed at communist sanctuaries and supply bases inside Cambodia. Only a small task force from 3rd Battalion, 506th Infantry, 101st Airborne, participated in the Cambodian incursion. On 3 May the battalion, operating with the US 4th Infantry Division, was ordered to join Operation 'Binh Tay I', the mission to pacify west Cambodia. Its mission was to move into the former PAVN and VC sanctuaries in the Prek Drang base camp area of Cambodia, west of Pleiku City, and there to find, fix and destroy enemy personnel and equipment. By 1000 hrs on 5 May, the battalion was en route to the LZs. As they approached several aircraft received ground fire, and for several elements, alternative LZs had to be utilised.

Over the coming five days the troops skirmished intermittently with the enemy, and unearthed significant caches of arms and foodstuffs. On the morning of 10 May, B Company discovered a hospital complex with numerous hootches and a multitude of foodstuff and two tons of rice, before engaging a large enemy force in a pitched battle that lasted nearly two days. Having fought off sustained attacks by two PAVN companies, the following day D and B Company linked up and secured an LZ for extraction of B Company, which had sustained eight killed and 28 wounded, to FSB Currahee. A later sweep of the contact area by Delta Company revealed the bodies of 47 PAVN KIA and an unconfirmed number of wounded.

Below: Members of the 3rd Battalion, 187th Infantry, 101st Airborne Division (Airmobile), join the children of Ap Uu Thoung hamlet in a game of baseball. The troopers are members of a Battalion Action Team involved in pacification operations in Phong Dieu District, north of Hue, 15 January 1970.

Another sizeable cache of weapons and ammunition was discovered on 12 May by C Company. Among the captured equipment were small arms, rockets, artillery rounds, and thousands of grenades and mines of various types and descriptions.

There were no major ground activities in the area, but the enemy continued to be engaged in small actions for the next four days. On 16 May, the remainder of 3rd Battalion, 506th Infantry, began redeploying from Cambodia, returning to FSB Wildcat over the border in Vietnam.

At the end of June the remaining ARVN and US troops pulled out of Cambodia, having achieved little at a heavy price. From here on, there was little fighting in South Vietnam to speak of as US forces began a phased withdrawal. Although it never again fought a major engagement, the 101st Airborne was still engaged in ground operations and continued to distinguish itself in the field.

Operation 'Jefferson Glenn'
Following the conclusion of Operation 'Texas Star' on 5 September 1970, the 101st Airborne undertook the last major US military operation of the conflict: 'Jefferson Glenn'. Three battalions were tasked with establishing FSBs in the coastal lowlands of Thua Thien. The objective was to shield Thua Thien and Quang Tri by patrolling the belts of PAVN rocket launch sites that threatened critical installations.

Operation 'Lam Son 719'
At the end of January 1971, with US ground forces now operating largely in a support role, South Vietnamese forces launched a cross-border attack, with 101st Airborne Division support, into the border area of Laos adjacent to South Vietnam that had for many years been controlled by the enemy. The objectives of 'Lam Son 719' (named for the ARVN commander) were to disrupt an ongoing PAVN supply build-up at Tchepone in Laos, sever the Ho Chi Minh trail and destroy enemy staging areas. It was also seen as an important test of the airmobile concept.

Beginning on 8 February, the unit assisted in the airlift of 17,000 troops of the 1st ARVN Infantry Division and 1st ARVN Airborne Division from bases established on the Khe Sanh Plain into landing zones to the north and south of Route Nine. From here they were to attack an estimated 22,000 PAVN troops. Aided by heavy US artillery and air strikes, by 10 February the troops had seized the initial objectives of the operation. Soon enemy pressure bogged down the ARVN advance, and poor weather and heavy air defence opposition began to limit the air support available to relieve the pressure. This allowed the PAVN time to bring in massive armour and troop reinforcements from North Vietnam, South

Above: The last major campaign conducted by the 101st Airborne Division (Airmobile) in Vietnam was providing massive air support to the ARVN invasion of Laos – Operation 'Lam Son 719' – to cut the Ho Chi Minh Trail from 30 January to 6 April 1971. In conjunction with Operation 'Dewey Canyon II', a major air assault of six ARVN infantry battalions and an armoured brigade task force was launched into Laos on 8 February with all the US Army aviation units under the operational command of the 101st Airborne with the divisional air cavalry squadron, 2nd Squadron, 17th Cavalry, to the fore. 'Lam Son 719' proved to be a disaster and the policy of Vietnamisation was dealt a severe blow. Against the most intense anti-aircraft defences of the war with hundreds of heavy machine guns and more than 200 weapons ranging from SU-23-2 23mm cannon to the KS19 100mm gun, the US Army aviation units suffered heavy losses with 108 helicopters destroyed and 618 damaged but over 164,000 sorties were flown during the 67-day operation.

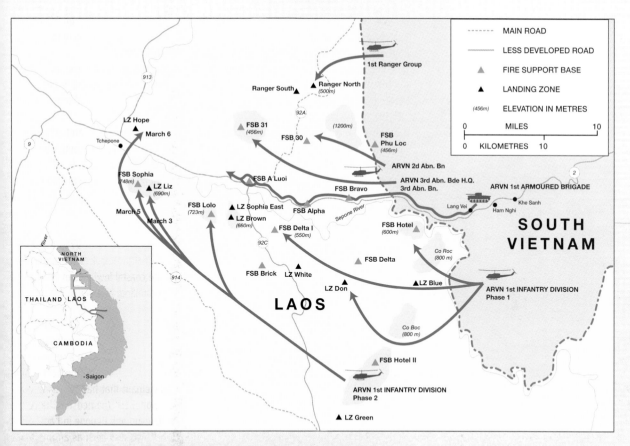

MAIN ROAD
LESS DEVELOPED ROAD
▲ FIRE SUPPORT BASE
▲ LANDING ZONE
(456m) ELEVATION IN METRES

0 — MILES — 10
0 — KILOMETRES — 10

1st Ranger Group

Ranger South ▲ Ranger North
(500m)

92A

LZ Hope
March 6
Tchepone

FSB 31
(456m)
FSB 30

(1200m)

FSB
Phu Loc
(456m)

ARVN 2d Abn. Bn

ARVN 3rd Abn. Bde H.Q.
3rd Abn. Bn.

ARVN 1st ARMOURED BRIGADE

FSB Sophia
(748m)
LZ Liz
(690m)

FSB A Luoi
FSB Bravo
FSB Alpha
Sepone River

Lang Vei
Ham Nghi
Khe Sanh

March 5

FSB Lolo
(723m)

LZ Sophia East
LZ Brown
(660m)

FSB Delta I
(550m)

FSB Hotel
(600m)

SOUTH
VIETNAM

March 3

92C

Co Roc
(800m)

FSB Brick
LZ White

FSB Delta

LZ Don
LZ Blue

ARVN 1st INFANTRY DIVISION
Phase 1

LAOS

Co Boc
(800m)

913

9

River

914

NORTH
VIETNAM

THAILAND LAOS

CAMBODIA
· Saigon

FSB Hotel II

ARVN 1st INFANTRY DIVISION
Phase 2

▲ LZ Green

Vietnam and other parts of Laos. By 25 February, the invading forces had discovered enemy supply bases more than a mile square and had cut a major POL pipeline. However, over the coming days resistance stiffened considerably, and furthermore, the weather hindered tactical air movement. After enemy infantry overran Fire Base 31 General Lam, unable to continue the advance along Highway 9, decided to gamble on using his airmobile support to attack the main objective of Tchepone with a series of rapid air assaults.

After a very effective preparation of the area by B-52s, on 6 March two infantry battalions were lifted by 120 UH-1s for 40 miles into LZ Hope, north of Tchepone. This massive combat assault was carried out in what was considered to be the most hostile air

Above: 101st Airborne's role in the incursion into 'Lam Son 719' Laos.

defence environment ever encountered in the entire war. (A Company, 101st Aviation Regiment, had been conducting covert insertions into Laos for some time, and was well appraised of the extensive air defences the enemy had built up in the border area.) Despite this, only one Huey was hit and it made a safe landing in the objective area. The PAVN immediately increased pressure in the area and it was decided to withdraw to the east before the weather worsened.

The last elements of the ARVN 1st Infantry Division were extracted on 21 March and the remaining ARVN forces withdrew back into South Vietnam over the next few days, pursued by a PAVN force numbering some 40,000 men. During the extraction extremely heavy anti-aircraft fire was encountered along routes to and from the ARVN fire bases.

When the operation officially ended on 9 April, it was estimated that thousands of tons of enemy ammunition, petroleum, oils and lubricants, and other supplies and equipment had been destroyed. But the cost was tremendous; the invading units had been driven out by and lost half of their force. US aircrew losses were 176 killed, 1,942 wounded and 42 missing. Helicopter losses were put at 108 destroyed and 618 damaged.

Following the debacle of 'Lam Son 719', until the withdrawal at the end of the year, the infantry units made only a few scattered contacts with the enemy; most of the fighting was done by division artillery and aviation assets. On 14 April the ARVN 1st Infantry Division, supported by the 101st Aviation Brigade, launched Operation 'Lam Son 720' in the A Shau Valley to cut enemy supply lines.

CONSOLIDATION and WITHDRAWAL

1 July–30 November 1971

During this period the Vietnamisation programme continued apace, sustaining the progressive withdrawal of US troops. Pressure on the enemy was maintained by US air strikes on targets in the North. On 11 July South Vietnam assumed full control of defence for the area immediately below the demilitarised zone, a process begun in 1969. Secretary of Defense Melvin R. Laird announced completion of Phase I of Vietnamisation a month later, meaning that the US relinquished all ground combat responsibilities to the Republic of Vietnam. By early November, US troop totals had dropped to 191,000.

The participation of US forces in ground combat operations had not ceased; the remaining US manoeuvre battalions were still conducting missions. Until the operation was terminated in August, the 101st Aviation Brigade continued to support 'Lam Son 720'. In Thua Thien Province, other divisional elements increasingly turned responsibility for Operation 'Jefferson Glen' over to the ARVN 1st Infantry Division. Following the close of the operation on 8 October, the 101st began stand-down procedures.

On 12 November 1971, President Nixon put all remaining US troops on a defensive status. Heavy air attacks on North Vietnam were staged in December while both sides exchanged peace proposals. In early January 1972, Nixon confirmed that US troop withdrawals would continue but promised that a force of 25,000–30,000 would remain in Vietnam until all American PoWs were released. Secretary of Defense Laird reported that Vietnamisation was progressing well and that US troops would not be reintroduced into Vietnam even in a military emergency. US troop strength in Vietnam dropped to 136,500 by 31 January 1972, to 119,600 by 29 February, and then to 95,500 by the end of March.

Over that winter, the 101st Airborne Division finally returned home to Fort Campbell, and by the spring of 1972 the Vietnam War was at a low ebb. Although it dragged on for three more years, this brought the curtain down on the 101st Airborne Division involvement. At the official homecoming ceremonies on 6 April 1972 at Fort Campbell, Vice President Spiro T. Agnew and Army Chief of Staff General William C. Westmoreland (who had welcomed the 101st to Vietnam in 1965) were there to welcome the division home.

Above: The 101st Airborne Division (Airmobile) alone lost 68 killed with 261 wounded and 17 missing in action during 'Lam Son 719'. In the words of the assistant division commander, Brigadier General Sidney B Berry Jr: 'Every airmobile operation, even single ship resupply and aeromedical evacuation missions, had to be planned and conducted as combat operations complete with fire plan, escorting armed helicopters, and plans for securing and recovering downed crews and helicopter.'

EQUIPMENT, MARKINGS AND CAMOUFLAGE

This chapter provides brief details of the insignia, clothing and equipment typically worn by 101st Airborne troops in Vietnam, and of some of the weapons, personal equipment and aircraft they used. It is by no means an attempt at a definitive guide, for which I would recommend one of the specialist texts listed in the Bibliography.

INSIGNIA

There are a large number of 'unofficial' insignia associated with the 101st Airborne and its sub-units, and as these are far too prolific to list individually, I have instead restricted the following information to those official insignia that were common to all troops. For information on the former see the bibliography.

In common with all airborne qualified troops, 101st troops wore a *distinctive insignia* on the front of the left curtain of the garrison cap, consisting of an embroidered white parachute and glider on a blue disk with a red border approximately 2.5 inches in diameter overall. During the Vietnam War these were made by a variety of manufacturers (and occasionally hand embroidered).

There is another insignia, a *distinctive unit insignia* (DUI) specific to the 101st Airborne, which is worn on the upper sleeve of their dress uniform troops. It is a black cloth shield on which is embroidered the head of a bald eagle (NVA and Viet Cong reputedly referred to the 101st as the 'Chickenmen' because of this). Immediately above and touching the shoulder sleeve insignia (SSI), there is a black arc tab inscribed with the legend 'AIRBORNE' in yellow letters. Above the 101st shoulder sleeve insignia was often worn individual unit symbols. The design of the SSI recalls one of the traditions of the old Wisconsin 'Iron Brigade', this state being the territory of the original 101st Division after the First World War. The black on the shield represents the 'Iron', and the eagle is the famous bird nicknamed 'Old Abe' that was carried into combat during the American Civil War by one of the Iron Brigade regiments.

Enlisted men wore a variation on this DUI design near front-of-left curtain on their Garrison Caps. This was a gold coloured metal and enamel device consisting of a medium blue disc; superimposed on this is a black demi-eagle with a white head, wing details and eye and a gold beak in downward flight emerging from a white cloud. Above is a gold scroll bearing the motto 'Rendezvous with Destiny' in black letters.

The *combat branch or combat support branch insignia*, which for the 101st was the crossed rifles of the infantry, was worn on both lower lapels of the officers' dress jacket. On both upper lapels a small gilt 'U.S.' distinguished them as officers in the US Army.

Enlisted men wore a badge on the left upper lapel denoting their branch, and on the

Above: With the divisional insignia emblazoned on the ground of Camp Eagle, members of the 101st Airborne Division parade during a change of command ceremony on 17 May 1969 when Maj Gen John M Wright Jr superseded Maj Gen Melvin Zais. Camp Eagle was situated north of Phu Bai between Hue and Da Nang on Route 1, the fabled 'Street Without Joy'.

Far Right: Men of Company C, 1st Battalion, 327th Infantry (Airborne), 1st Brigade, 101st Airborne Division (Separate), carefully negotiate a stream in search of the elusive enemy during Operation 'Geronimo I' on 19 November 1966. The nearest trooper is equipped with the recently introduced Lightweight Rucksack that was standardised in November 1965 and issued to troops in Vietnam during 1966. The water resistant nylon bag and tubular aluminium frame weighed just three pounds. It featured one large compartment and three external pockets with twice the carrying capacity as its forerunner; it also had attachment straps for other items such as the one-quart plastic canteen shown here.

right upper lapel a small, round badge with the embossed legend 'U.S.' to distinguish them as soldiers in the US Army.

Variations on the US Army eagle insignia for general and warrant officers, and enlisted men, were worn on the garrison cap and on the front of the left breast pocket.

Rank insignia for both officers and enlisted men followed the pattern and positioning prescribed for all US troops on their dress and field uniforms: that is on the upper sleeve of both dress and field jackets for enlisted men, and on officer's shoulder epaulettes. All officers and NCOs also wore rank insignia near front-of-left curtain on their garrison caps. General, commissioned and warrant officers' caps had an edge braid of metallic gold, interwoven metallic gold and black, or interwoven metallic silver and black, respectively, and enlisted men an edge braid of black.

Medals, Combat and Special Skill Badges. Although not all men who served with the 101st were so qualified, those men entitled to Army Parachutist Wings wore them on the right lower side of the left breast pocket flap. On the dress uniform, medal ribbons were stitched in rows immediately above this flap, and in the same position above the right breast pocket, the unit citation ribbons (for a list of these see Appendix A). Above the medal ribbons on the left, the soldiers pinned their combat badges.

Finally, each man had a name badge on his right breast pocket flap, a subdued olive green version of which was produced for field jackets.

Field Uniform (Subdued) Insignia. On officers' and enlisted men's field uniforms, 'subdued' versions of some of these insignia were stitched. The insignia was produced in the same colour cloth as the uniform, and embroidered in black stitching. Officers wore the 'crossed rifles' combat branch patch on the right lapel. All ranks wore subdued name tags, rank insignia, Combat and Special Skill Badges (including Army Parachutist Wings), but in place of the medal ribbons there was a patch bearing the legend 'US ARMY'. Unique to the 101st Airborne was the subdued distinctive unit insignia patch that they were permitted to wear on the upper left shoulder.

Right: Laden down with equipment, a trooper of Company C, 2D Battalion, 502D Infantry (Airborne), 1st Brigade, 101st Airborne Division (Separate), treads carefully through a stream ever watchful for booby traps as his unit conducts a patrol in the 'boonies' during Operation 'Harrison' on 27 February 1966. Of interest, he is carrying several different types of hand grenades with the old World War II Mark IIA1 Fragmentation Grenade or 'pineapple' on his webbing belt next to an M8 white smoke and on his shoulder harness an M18 coloured smoke grenade. Under his left arm he is carrying a bag of demolition stores or M18A1 Claymore mines and under his right arm, next to his M16 rifle, boot socks stuffed with individual C-ration cans and other items of personal storage.

Right: A member of Company A, 1st Battalion, 327th Infantry (Airmobile), 1st Brigade, 101st Airborne Division (Airmobile), is presented with a medal by Major General Thomas Tarpley, the divisional commander, at Camp Eagle on 2 January 1972 during a stand down ceremony as the 'Screaming Eagles' return to the United States as part of Increment X of the US Army withdrawal from Vietnam. Divisional Headquarters closed on 10 March 1972 after 1,573 days in country as a full division. It suffered 4,011 killed in action – the third highest of any division in Vietnam – 18,259 wounded in action and its members were awarded 20 Medals of Honor.

Below: Happiness is a cold LZ – troopers of the 101st Airborne Division (Airmobile) rush to the treeline as their UH-1H Huey touches down in a jungle clearing; the trooper on the left is carrying an M19 60mm mortar tube. This weapon had a range of one mile and was capable of firing up to 30 rounds a minute, if sufficient ammunition was to hand. The total complement of helicopters in an airmobile division in Vietnam was 434 ranging from the tiny OH-13S Sioux to the gigantic CH-54 Skycrane.

CLOTHING

Dress uniform of the 101st Airborne Division was the standard US-Army-pattern uniform of the time, which consisted of a dark green, single-breast, waisted tunic and matching pleated trousers, with appropriate parade insignia, medal ribbons and so forth. In Vietnam it was rarely worn by troops except when on R&R.

Field uniform. In 1965 the US Army was still issuing the 'green sateen' field uniform to its troops. However, the demands of fighting in the hot and humid climate of Vietnam created a need for a different type of uniform, and a new pattern tunic and trousers were adopted. This older pattern tunic had two square breast and two lower pockets fastened by press studs. It had a distinctive round-cut collar.

These items were replaced in Vietnam by a new uniform based on the Second World War Para uniform, consisting of a tropical jungle jacket and matching trousers. Both jacket and trousers were made of tightly woven, quick-drying, wind-resistant poplin or Rip-Stop cotton fabric in olive drab army shade 107. They provided good protection against the sun, insects and other tropical hazards. Also, the loosely fitted garments provided body-heat ventilation and moisture dissipation.

The tunic was produced in three standard patterns, with differences of detail. All had two chest bellows pockets and two lower bellows pockets. In the field, tunic sleeves were commonly rolled up or cut off.

Three patterns of matching jungle trousers were issued. They had two front pockets, two hip pockets, two bellows cargo leg pockets, a small pocket inside the left cargo pocket for a survival kit, and draw cords at the bottom of the trouser legs. Although cool and comfortable, the trousers had a tendency to rip, especially at the knee.

Also issued was an olive-drab cotton T-shirt and a cotton–sateen utility fatigue shirt. The shirt was a shrink-resistant, heat-retentive and moisture-resistant garment with full-length sleeves, knitted cuffs and buttoned collar closure in olive drab.

Left: War is 90% tedium and 10% terror with hours of waiting for nothing to happen – Pfc Edward Horton spends his time reading a book while waiting to undertake a combat air assault during Operation 'Cook' on 8 September 1967. Attached to his M1956 Individual Load Carrying Equipment is an M26A1 fragmentation grenade and beside him is an M1 Steel Helmet with Leaf Pattern Camouflage Cover. The M1 helmet of paratroopers was fitted with the M1-C Parachutist's Liner with its distinctive web A-straps and chincup. Typically he wears his wristwatch attached to his OG107 utility shirt so as to avoid chafing and sores around his wrist in the hot and humid conditions of Vietnam.

BOOTS

Five types of combat boot were used in Vietnam. The standard all-leather combat boots that were first issued proved to be totally useless for fighting in the steamy jungles and swamps, and a purpose-designed jungle boot was soon introduced. This was manufactured in four patterns, all with leather and nylon sole and heel box, and canvas uppers and ventilation holes to speed drying. Air crew and chopper pilots tended to wear the older style right through the war because of fears about the nylon jungle boot sole melting in a fire.

Because of the numerous instances of immersion or trench foot among soldiers in Vietnam, particularly among those troops operating in the Delta for extended periods, 'comfort shoes' (otherwise known as 'bivouac slippers') were issued. The comfort shoe was constructed of an OG-106 nylon and rubber sole. They were fastened by an elastic velcro band, with two lace-up holes underneath the velcro band should this break. Comfort shoes were designed to be small and light enough to be folded up and stuffed into a pocket when not in use.

CLOTHING ACCESSORIES

I have omitted mundane but essential items such as socks and underwear. However, I include three items because they are commonly seen in period photographs; first is the tropical combat neckerchief, a popular item that was essentially a sweat cloth of highly absorbent, dark green cotton in army shade 409. This cloth was useful for wiping perspiration and dirt from the brow and hands, and for cleaning weapons and ammunition. It was worn over or around the head in a variety of bandanna, cravat and sweatband styles. There was also a knitted wool scarf, a seamless tubular scarf with reinforced ends that doubled as a cap or hand muff. The standard issue green field towel was also often worn around the neck to wipe the face free of sweat and protect the neck and shoulders from the chaffing of yoke straps or shouldered equipment.

HEADGEAR

Based on the design of the WW2-pattern M1 helmet, the M1 of the 1960s had a lower profile but was otherwise unchanged. It was quite heavy to wear, particularly in the humid jungle of Vietnam. The two-part chinstrap was typically fixed up around the rear of the helmet. A helmet liner with nape strap or neckband was attached to the inside of the helmet and a reversible helmet cover to the outside, on which troops often wrote personal graffiti. For additional camouflage, the cover contained small slots for inserting natural foliage. An elasticated helmet band was designed to help hold the foliage in place, but was more commonly used to fasten field dressings, cigarettes, toilet paper, insect repellent or a spare magazine to the helmet so as to keep them dry and readily accessible.

There was also a standard issue tropical hat, made of either cotton poplin or rip-stop fabric. The hat featured an adjustable chinstrap, foliage loops and ventilation eyelets around the crown. An insect net was issued with it, but not often used. A visored, baseball style fatigue cap, made of polyester and dyed olive green, was available but was very unpopular with troops. Australian-style bush hats, cowboy-style hats and other non-regulation headgear produced locally were commonly worn.

Above: Booby traps – improvised explosive devices (IEDs) – were one of the greatest fears for the infantryman on the ground from the simple 'toe-popper' made from a single rifle round to the command-detonated US Air Force unexploded aerial bomb. All wrought havoc and destruction without a moment's notice to foot patrols and vehicles. This training patrol at the Screaming Eagle Replacement School at Bien Hoa remains prone and watchful as the point man investigates a suspected IED, affording us among other things, with an excellent view of his combat boots.

Below: A Radio Telephone Operator (RTO) checks out his AN/PRC-25 FM radios in the field. The M1956 Load Carrying Equipment was configured to accommodate the Electrical Equipment Harness that incorporated the radio. Note the Spares Bag attached to the left of the radio that contained the seven-section long-range 'fishpole' antenna and a spare handset. Although highly reliable, the main shortcoming of the 'Prick 25' was its lack of a scrambler/descrambler device for secure transmissions, although this was rectified with a modified model that became the AN/PRC-77. Generally, communications security was poor in the US Army during the Vietnam war and many operations were compromised by the enemy's successful use of radio intercepts. Note, too, the helmets and other personal equipment on the grass beside him, and his 'Screaming Eagles' shoulder patch.

Right: Men of Company L, 75th (Ranger) Infantry, take a break during Operation 'Bushmaster' in support of the 501st Infantry (Airmobile), 101st Airborne Division (Airmobile), while conducting a search and destroy mission northwest of Phu Bai in the vicinity of Fire Support Base Rifle during August 1971. On 1 February 1969, all existing US Army LURP units were redesignated as Rangers and were assigned to the 75th Infantry.

Below Right: Pfc Tony Baker and Plt Sgt Fred Brander of the 1st Brigade, 101st Airborne Division (Separate), set explosive charges to enemy equipment left behind by the Viet Cong during Operation 'Van Buren' on 3 February 1966. The operation lasted for 34 days from 19 January to 21 February 1966 and resulted in 679 enemy casualties.

Below: A classic image of the infantryman at war as a small unit patrol confers during a typical operation conducted by the 101st Airborne Division (Airmobile) in Vietnam. Two of the troopers are draped with 200-round belts of disintegrating link 7.62mm ammunition to serve the squad M60 machine gun team; the men at left and right have their M16A1 rifles to hand and carry extra magazines in cotton bandoliers. The M193 Rifle Bandolier held seven 20-round M16 magazines and four bandoliers per man were typical to give a standard ammunition total of 560 rounds.

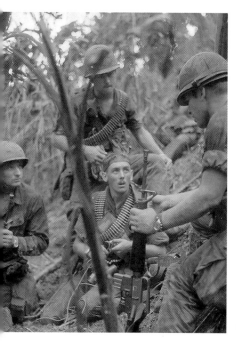

INDIVIDUAL EQUIPMENT

Combat troops were issued with basic, and more specialised, items of load-carrying equipment in or on which they carried such items as they needed to shelter, eat, fight and survive in combat. Until 1967 the M1956 pattern kit continued to be issued, with improvements in the detail of certain items. After this time a modernised version designed specially for Vietnam – the M1967 Load Carrying Equipment (LCE) – was introduced. The new equipment was essentially the same but replaced metal with plastic and canvas with nylon, which unlike the canvas was mildew resistant. The M1967 LCE did not entirely replace the earlier kit; the two were often mixed together to form composite webbing, since both types were fully compatible with each other.

The basic item was the pistol belt, to which were attached all other items. The M1967 Davis belt was essentially the same as the M1956 pattern, but was produced in both canvas and nylon and had the quick release 'Davis buckle'. The weight of kit mounted on the belt was distributed to the shoulders by means of suspenders (yoke straps), which attached from the front of the pistol belt to the buttpack (see below) or else directly to the back of the pistol belt to form an H shaped load-carrying system. The M1967 pattern suspenders had two fasteners to allow the buttpack to be mounted higher, and were made of padded nylon. There were also metal loops on each suspender for the attachments of small items. A single yoke version was produced.

To the belt were attached universal ammo pouches, the standard ammunition pouch for the Colt M16 magazine. The M1956 pouch was made of canvas, and there were carriers either side for grenades. A smaller canvas pouch was issued in late 1967 to early 1968. This was designed for easier access to the shorter M16 20-round magazine. M1967 ammo pouches were similar to this small version of the M1956 universal ammo pouch, but were made of nylon and had a quick release closure.

To strap his sleeping bag or poncho with liner rolled inside to the suspenders the soldier used the sleeping carrier. This complicated set of straps, also called 'spagette straps', was manufactured in canvas.

Below the sleeping carrier he attached the buttpack (also called the fanny pack), which was used to carry spare items of clothing, rations, cooking utensils and so forth. It has wings of canvas that fold inwards. The carry straps are underneath and clips on the rear attach it to the pistol belt. If required, the suspenders can be attached to the top through riveted holes on the flaps. An improved version issued from 1961 was a little larger and lined in plastic, and an adapter allowed the user to strap the buttpack higher on the shoulders, but neither design was particularly satisfactory.

In 1965 the design of the 'lightweight tropical rucksack' was standardised and it was issued in the following year to replace the M1956 and M1961 buttpacks. It consisted of a water-resistant nylon bag with one large compartment and three external pockets. This was fixed to a tubular aluminium frame. However, the rucksack prevents items being worn on the pistol belt, thus water canteens and first aid kits are located elsewhere, such as on the rucksack frame itself. A larger version known as the tropical rucksack was used, but soldiers in Vietnam generally found the X-frame to be uncomfortable over long periods of wear. More popular was the issue ARVN rucksack, originally produced for the South Vietnam Rangers and based on a North Vietnamese army pack. It became popular with US personnel because of its light weight and generous capacity. It was manufactured as a cotton duck pack with two external pockets and mounted on a sprung metal X frame, which kept the load high and away from the user's back.

Other items of belt kit included;

Compass pouch. A small pouch designed to hold either a lensatic compass or a field dressing.

Above: M114A1 155mm howitzers are prepared for action at Fire Support Base Ripcord situated in the A Shau Valley to support the operations of the 2nd Battalion, 506th Infantry (Airmobile) 101st Airborne Division (Airmobile) against the base areas of the 324th NVA Division during the ferocious fighting of July 1970. At this time, the 101st Airborne Division (Airmobile) was supported by two battalions of 155mm howitzers – the 2nd Battalion, 11th Artillery (155mm) and 1st Battalion, 39th Artillery (155mm). The latter was a self-propelled unit originally equipped with M109 155mm howitzers and latterly M107 175mm guns and M110 8-inch howitzers. Accordingly these M114A1 howitzers belonged to the 2nd Battalion, 11th

Artillery, – the Dragon Regiment – which arrived in Vietnam on 13 December 1966 and served with II Field Force Artillery and then Task Force Oregon before being assigned to the 101st Airborne Division (Airmobile) on 10 June 1968. During the summer of 1970 the US firebases were tempting targets to the enemy and the NVA repeatedly bombarded and attacked Fire Support Base Ripcord. In one three-week period 61 troopers of the 101st were killed and a further 345 wounded. Because of the heavy enemy pressure, FSB Ripcord was abandoned on 23 July with the loss of one CH-47 Chinook and damage to eight others out of a total of 14 involved in the evacuation.

Right: Members of Battery C, 2nd Battalion, 320th Artillery (105mm) (Airborne), 1st Brigade, 101st Airborne Division (Separate), fire their M102 105mm howitzer at maximum elevation from Fire Support Base Bastogne in support of combat operations on 16 April 1968. The M102 was specially designed for airborne and airmobile formations and was 1,500 pounds lighter than the M101A1. It could pivot through 360 degrees for faster engagement times.

Right: 'Hang it in the tube' – the crew of an M29 81mm mortar stand by for their next fire mission during a 101st Airborne Division (Airmobile) operation in February 1966. The M29 had a maximum range of 3,500 yards and a good crew could fire 30 rounds a minute but a normal sustained rate of fire was five or six a minute. There were three 81mm mortars per company and each had a six-man crew. The weapon fired High Explosive, White Phosphorous and illuminating rounds. An HE round weighed over 7lb so carrying rounds in the 'boonies' was a back-breaking task and mortars were often concentrated in firebases to provide immediate fire support to units in the field via an FOO (Forward Observation Officer) operating with the troops on the ground.

One-quart canteen and cover. A felt-lined, cotton-duck water canteen cover and polyethylene canteen, of which two were commonly carried. The M1967 pattern was fully nylon and had a small pouch for purifying tablets. The canteen fitted into a canteen cup and the cup inside the canteen cover. There was also a two-quart collapsible canteen in two patterns, consisting of a square, moulded-vinyl bladder and an M1910-pattern cap with chain. The bladder flattened when empty. The canteen could only be carried in a matching cover on the belt or in other positions, and took up a lot of space.

Entrenching tool and case. Until replaced, the M1951 pattern E-tool was used as the standard folding entrenchment tool. It had a wooden haft and could be adjusted to different angles. It was an excellent weapon and archaeological tool for digging trenches and filling sandbags. A heavier variant on this had an added pick. The 1967 pattern tri-folding E-tool was a great improvement on the old wooden-hafted E-tool. It had a hollow, triangular-shaped handle and single shovel blade, with one edge sharpened for cutting and the other serrated for digging. The blade could be adjusted to different angles in the same way as the M1951 E-tool. It folded twice for carrying and was stored in a stiff plastic case, which had slide attachments which allowed it to be mounted anywhere on the belt.

M1916 Pistol holster. Officers and chopper pilots were issued with the M1916 pistol holster, the standard black leather holster with 'US' imprinted on the flap. There was also a shoulder holster.

Shelter

For shelter on operations each soldier would carry a *half-man pup tent,* a tent pole that could be split into three sections and tent pegs. The tent was basically a panel with triangular flaps made in olive-green, water-repellent, mildew-resistant cotton duck. Two of these could be buttoned together to form a complete tent. In the event that the tent could not be used, a more immediate form of shelter was available in the *poncho.* The early item was in olive-green rubberised fabric, and very heavy when wet; when worn as a garment in humid Vietnam, it was also hot and sweaty. However, a useful feature of the poncho was that two could be snapped together to make a temporary shelter or 'hooch'. It was also commonly used as a ground sheet or a makeshift stretcher. A lightweight poncho, identical to the standard poncho but fabricated from a nylon-based fabric with polyurethane coating, was produced.

To sleep on the soldier had an olive green inflatable *air mattress* the same size and shape as the sleeping bag. It also doubled as a float for carrying items across streams and flooded land. Conditions permitting, the troops may also have used *jungle hammocks* to sleep on. The US Army's standard jungle hammock was made of water-repellent treated nylon supported by quarter-inch-thick polyester draw cords. The first soldiers to Vietnam had a heavy wool *blanket,* which became even heavier when wet and proved totally unsuitable. This was replaced by the *poncho liner,* a quick-drying, lightweight, quilted item made of rip-stop parachute fabric. This could be laced into the poncho to make a makeshift sleeping bag, although a purpose designed *sleeping bag* was also issued.

Eating

In the field the soldier used his self-contained aluminium mess canteen and utensils to prepare the food and drink contained in the individual C-ration meal. The 'Meal Combat Individual' consisted of a box containing a main meal (pork and beans, spaghetti and meatballs etc.), a B2 unit (crackers, candy, cheese), a dessert (canned fruit, pound-cake) and an accessory pack (pictured). The accessory pack contained a P-38 can opener, hot drink, gum, matches, toilet paper, salt, sugar, a plastic spoon and a small pack of cigarettes. LRRP units were issued with their own special ration packs.

Below: Pfc Oliver Crews struggles with an M79 grenade launcher during training at the Screaming Eagle Replacement Training School at Bien Hoa. Note the sighting mechanism above the barrel that allowed accurate fire out to a range of 400m. The weapon fired High Explosive, Smoke, Flechette and parachute illuminating rounds.

Medical

The standard medical kit was the Medical Instrument Supply Set, also known as a 'Unit One' bag. It was a 3-compartment bag made of heavy canvas, or of rubberised cotton after 1968. Nylon bags appeared in the early 1970s. Typical contents would include different sizes of dressings and bandages, an emergency instrument set, blood volume expanders, aspirin and anti-malaria tablets. Medical Bag No. 5 was a rectangular canvas rucksack with a large internal space for storing all the medical supplies a platoon would need, including an emergency surgical instrument set. It was issued with a Waterproof Carrier, which was produced in rubberised cotton, or nylon duck after 1967.

Gasmasks and fragmentation vests

CS and other gases were used extensively for tunnel-clearing, and two types of gas mask were issued. The first was the M17 Field Protective Gas Mask, a rubberised mask worn over the face to protect the face, eyes and respiratory tract. It was carried in a bag with straps that could be attached around the left leg, and came complete with spare eye lenses. The later M17A1 had a drinking tube in the front of the mask, which could be attached to the one-quart canteen by means of a special cap. A rubberised cotton mask hood could be worn over the gas mask to protect head neck and shoulders.

Body armour came in a variety of forms, all of them designed to protect the core of the body and vital organs. Given the high proportion of injuries inflicted by mines and booby traps, and the weight of the armour, many troops scorned its use. The most common was the M1952 fragmentation jacket, developed during the Korean War and used right through the Vietnam War. The vest contained a filler of semi-flexible layers of ballistic nylon cloth, with a quarter-inch layer of sponge rubber over the ribs and shoulders. This served as a shock-absorbing layer to alleviate contusions and fractures from the impact of missiles. The vest closed with a full-length zipper and could be adjusted by laced closures at both sides. It had two chest pockets, shoulder straps and two rows of web hangers for grenades and other equipment.

Above Left: With the divisional insignia on the pilot's door, a wounded trooper of the 1st Battalion, 506th Infantry (Airmobile), 3rd Brigade, 101st Airborne Division (Airmobile), is helped aboard an 'Eagle Dust Off' UH-1H during an operation near Hue. The 'medevac' helicopters were a great boost to morale for US troops in the frustrating type of warfare fought in Vietnam where the enemy could strike at any moment to cause casualties and then slip away into the hinterland before any significant retaliation was possible.

Above: Troopers of the 101st Airborne Division (Airmobile) progress along a chow line at Fire Support Base Victory near the Montagnard village of Mai Loc in the Central Highlands on 16 October 1969. Note the shoulder sleeve insignia of the Screaming Eagle. Most units produced a subdued version of their insignia but this was not favoured in the 'Airborne' and the 101st continued to display the full colour version. Units took great pride in their insignia and their titles such as the Screaming Eagles but equally units were highly disparaging of others – such as the nickname given to the 101st of the 'Vomiting Vultures' or 'Puking Buzzards'. To the NVA, the 101st were known as the 'Chicken Men' as few Vietnamese had ever seen an eagle.

Left: A UH-1H aeromedical helicopter brings in wounded members of Company D, 2nd Battalion, 502nd Infantry (Airborne), 101st Airborne Division, to Fire Support Base Berchtesgaden during Operation 'Somerset Plain' in August 1968. The aeromedical helicopters of the 101st Airborne Division (Airmobile) were attached to the 326th Medical Battalion and were known as 'Eagle Dust Off' whose unit motto was 'If we can't nobody else can.' (See also photo and caption on page 79.)

Right: Medical staff of the 326th Medical Battalion load a wounded trooper of the 2nd Battalion, 327th Infantry (Airborne) into an ambulance for transfer from the medical clearing station to a filed hospital. It was the proud boast of the medical facilities that if one was hit in the field it was possible to get the wounded man to a field hospital within 20 minutes; if seriously injured to a base hospital in Japan within 12 hours and if killed, the body would be home in a week thanks to the 'KIA Travel Bureau' of Graves Registration. Note the old French watchtower in the background.

Right: The crewchief of a UH-1H hangs on to the electrical hoist as he guides his pilot out of a tight Pick-up Zone as the aeromedical evacuation helicopter extracts wounded troopers of the 101st Airborne Division (Airmobile) during an operation near the DMZ on 16 October 1969.

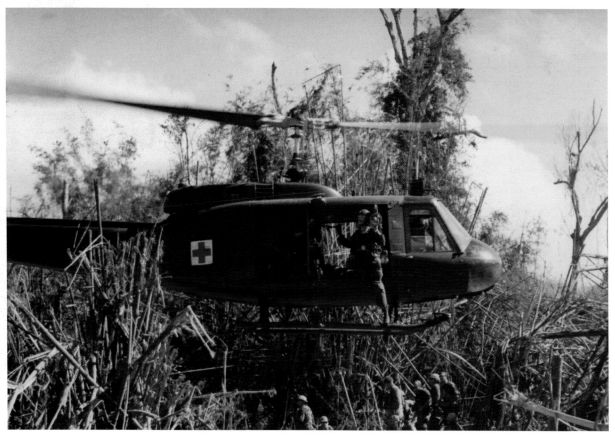

The M1969 fragmentation jacket was basically an upgraded version of the M1952, with extra ballistic nylon layers and a semi-stiff three-quarter inch collar with three layers of ballistic filling, providing protection to the neck. In 1966 'body armour, small arms protective, ground troops' was introduced in an attempt to provide the soldier with a vest that not only acted as a fragmentation vest, but also protected against small arms fire. It consisted of a flexible shell of ballistic nylon felt, with pockets on both the front and rear to accommodate form-fitting ceramic composite armour plates. These plates had integrated web straps allowing them to be worn independently of the vest, and vice versa. However, with all the armour in place, the vest was very heavy, weighing around 22lb.

Weapons maintenance equipment and accessories

Basic accessories were the rifle sling and bipod. Later in the war certain troops were issued with 'Starlight' scopes. Perhaps the most important item of maintenance equipment was the cleaning kit, the contents of which varied according to weapon. Typically this contained: cleaning rod set, bore brushes, chamber brushes, a double-ended plastic toothbrush, cloth cleaning patches, a bottle of bore cleaner, compound solvent and a bottle of light small arms (LSA) gun oil. Miscellaneous items were carried in the *small arms accessories case* and *paratrooper's weapons case*.

In addition, there was a plethora of specialist equipment for machine guns and mortar crews, much of which had to be carried into the field. Machine gun crews, for example, had a special case for the spare barrel and gloves to change it.

In addition each man would most likely carry the following items in his equipment: sewing kit; personal hygiene kit; flashlight with a compartment containing coloured lens filters that could be attached to the front of the flashlight; sunburn cream; insect repellent; foot powder; first aid packet/field dressing; purification tablets (Puri-tabs).

WEAPONS

- *Pistols.* These included the M-1911A1 Colt .45in automatic pistol and L9A1 9mm (.45in) FN Browning High Power
- *Submachine guns.* The M1A1 Thompson .45 in, M3A1 .45in 'grease gun' and Model 45 9mm 'Carl Gustav' were used in the early part of the conflict
- *Rifles and carbines.* The first weapon issued to US troops in Vietnam was the M1 'Garand', a 0.3in self-loading rifle essentially unchanged from that carried by US infantrymen in the Second World War. This was replaced by the M-14, which fired the 7.62mm NATO cartridge, and subsequently by the M-16 5.56mm Assault Rifle (but only after some major teething troubles). A shorter carbine version designated CAR-15 was also issued.
- *Grenades and rifle grenades.* The Mk2, M26 and M61 were the standard Anti-Personnel Defensive Hand Grenades. The Mk2 could be launched by rifle. The M-79 was a dedicated shoulder-fired 40 mm grenade launcher; the M203 40mm grenade launcher attached to the underside of the M-16 barrel.
- *Machine guns, medium and heavy.* The M-60 7.62mm GPMG was the standard medium machine gun. Much loved by the troops for its impressive rate of fire, this weapon was also mounted on choppers and vehicles. Although best in the hands of a skilled gunner, for static base defence the 1919 vintage M2 .50-cal heavy barrel was highly prized.
- *Anti-armour weapons.* Although North Vietnamese armour was rarely encountered, it was occasionally engaged with anti-armour weapons. The most common was the man portable M72 66mm HEAT light anti-armour weapon (LAW). Although designed for use

Below: SP4 Robert Canfield of Company B, 1st Battalion, 327th Infantry (Airborne), 1st Brigade, 101st Airborne Division, (Separate), cleans his M16A1 rifle before going on patrol during Operation 'Wheeler' near Chu Lai in November 1967. The M16 required constant servicing for reliable operation in the field as a fellow trooper of the 101st, Pfc William Austin discovered during Operation 'Wheeler'. As he crossed a paddyfield he was charged by a water buffalo, one of the most irascible and dangerous animals encountered in Vietnam, scattering everyone in the patrol except Austin who was rooted to the spot. As he lifted his M16 to his shoulder, the buffalo knocked the weapon from his hands as it thundered by only to turn around and charge again. Retrieving his rifle from the mud, he pulled the trigger but nothing happened. Quickly clearing the jam, he fired again and the enraged animal fell pinning Austin to the ground. He screamed at his cowering colleagues to do something to which came the response – 'Olé!' On 18 November 1967, the 1st Brigade rejoined the 'Screaming Eagles' after the arrival of the division in November 1967. The brigade then lost its designation of 1st Brigade, 101st Airborne Division (Separate) and reverted to 1st Brigade.

against soft-skinned and lightly armoured vehicles, this proved particularly effective against bunkers. The standard infantry recoilless rifle was the M67 90 mm, a highly effective weapon that could be either tripod or vehicle mounted. In the former configuration, three men could carry it, but it was heavy and awkward and generally relegated to base defence. The first generation of aerial rocket artillery and some gunships employed the SS-11 wire-guided missile, which was flown to the target (usually a bunker) using a small joystick. Later in the war the impressive M151E2 127mm TOW was deployed. This was a wire-guided semi-automatic command-to-line of-sight-system with a high-explosive anti-tank (HEAT) warhead.

• *Mortars.* These ranged in size from the M2 and M19 60 mm tubes, which were generally only used by reconnaissance teams, to the M1 and M29 81 mm (3.2 in), which were the standard US Army medium mortars and provided a significant amount of readily available firepower to the manoeuvring infantry. The 4.2 in M30 was also employed, but because of its size and weight this was left in the base camps or fire bases for static defence.

HELICOPTERS

Helicopters used by the US Army were generally classified as 'utility', 'attack', 'observation', 'cargo' and 'heavy' – designations which are largely self-explanatory. The types used by aviation units assigned to the 101st Airborne are detailed below.

One of these aircraft in particular must be highlighted. That is the *Bell UH-1*, originally introduced in the utility role and, in the later of its many versions, used as to provide aerial rocket artillery and as a gunship. It was largely because of the Vietnam War that this aircraft became the second most numerous aircraft since the Second World War, and there was no significant clash of arms on the soil of South Vietnam in which the UH-1 did not participate. Crewed by three and designed to accommodate up to 15 troops (although this was regularly exceeded) it provided the backbone of US Army airmobility in Vietnam and was the helicopter most widely used by the 101st Airborne.

The other major type was the Bell *AH-1G Cobra*. This purpose-built gunship was the mainstay of the 101st's aerial rocket artillery units. It was operated by a crew of two sitting in tandem in a sleek fuselage with stub wings, with the gunner in the front position. Its weapons included 7.62 mm mini-guns, 40-mm grenade launchers, 20-mm cannon, anti-tank missiles and various rockets.

The observation and scout units flew the *Hughes OH-6 Cayuse*, a six-seater aircraft with a distinctive egg-shaped fuselage introduced in 1967 to replace the Bell H-13 Sioux. The OH-6 was itself eventually replaced by the *Bell OH-58A Kiowa*.

Two much larger helicopters were used by the 101st Airborne for heavy lifts. The more common was the Boeing Vertol *CH-47 Chinook*, a large tandem-rotor transport able to seat 44 fully-equipped troops or carry modest vehicles and artillery. A, B and C models were in use in the Vietnam conflict. Chinooks could fly in as slung loads all the

Above: Smoking can seriously damage your health but then so can a firefight with the 24th NVA Regiment as encountered by the 1st Battalion, 327th Infantry (Airborne), 1st Brigade, 101st Airborne Division (Separate), on the morning of 7 June 1966 during Operation 'Hawthorne' that was conducted to protect the Ruff Puff outpost of Tou Morong near Dak To and pre-empt an NVA offensive in Kontum Province. During its early years of service with the US Army the M16 5.56mm assault rifle suffered serious problems in the field with repeated stoppages that was attributed to inadequate cleaning and servicing by the troops. These problems led to the introduction of an improved model known as the M16A1 and thereafter it proved to be an excellent weapon for jungle operations although meticulous cleaning procedures remained vital.

Right: One of the particular aviation assets of the airmobile divisions in the Vietnam war was the aerial rocket battalion within the Division Artillery. Equipped with UH-1 or AH-1 Cobra armed helicopters, the batteries provided the closest fire support to the ground troops, often delivering their 2.75-inch rockets within metres of friendly forces to suppress enemy fire and eliminate their positions. In the 101st, such fire support was provided by the 4th Battalion, 77th Artillery (Aerial Rocket) known as the 'Dragons'.

Below Right: A CH-47C Chinook of the 159th Aviation Battalion (Assault Support Helicopter) hovers over the POL point at Fire Support Base Tomahawk as it releases an underslung load of fuel bladders on 10 April 1971. Introduced in March 1968, the CH-47C featured an improved transmission and uprated engines that doubled the load and range of the original A model that first saw action with the 1st Cavalry Division (Airmobile) in September 1965. The white triangle on the forward rotor pylon indicates Company B – callsign Varsity – within the aviation battalion; A being a red triangle – The Pachyderms – and C blue which rejoiced in the callsign of Playtex as they provided 'support' for the division; indeed, one Chinook had a large pink bra painted underneath the fuselage. Company B had originally requested the callsign 'Mother Truckers' but the army deemed this to be unseemly.

Below: A striking image of the concept of airmobility as troopers of Company C, 1st Battalion, 327th Infantry (Airmobile), 1st Brigade, 101st Airborne climb aboard a UH-1H to return to Fire Support Base Birmingham on 15 April 1971. The helicopter provided extraordinary mobility in the area warfare of Vietnam, capable of inserting troops over scores of miles.

air-portable guns, ammunition and supply packages used in Vietnam, as well as such mundane items as trucks of drinking water. The other heavy lift helicopter was the Sikorsky CH-54 'Tarhe' (Flying Crane) aircraft. Almost the entire US Army inventory of this aircraft saw combat duty in Vietnam, carrying bulldozers, graders and light armour as slung loads, picking up and repositioning artillery, and also rescuing over 380 downed aircrew.

Among secondary US Army types in Vietnam were small numbers of older helicopters, including the Bell *OH-13 'Sioux'* and *OH-23 'Raven'* observation helicopters, the Piasecki (Vertol) *CH-21 'Shawnee'* and Sikorsky *CH-34 'Choctaw'* (designated the UH-34 'Dog' by USMC).

AVIATION UNITS

Detailed below are the aviation units assigned to 101st Airborne Division, with their call signs, aircraft type, and operating base.

158th Aviation Bn
HQ and HQ Company 158th Aviation Bn. 'Lightning' UH-1 Evans
A Company 158th Aviation Bn 'Ghost Riders' UH-1 Evans
B Company 158th Aviation Bn. 'Lancers' UH-1 Evans
C Company 158th Aviation Bn. 'Phoenix' UH-1 Evans
D Company 158th Aviation Bn. 'Redskins' AH-1G Evans

101st Aviation Bn
HQ and HQ Company 101st Aviation Bn. 'Mustang' UH-1 Eagle
A Company 101st Aviation Bn. 'Comanchero' UH-1 Eagle
B Company 101st Aviation Bn 'Kingsmen' UH-1 Eagle
B Company Gunships 101st Aviation Bn. 'Kingsmen' UH-1 Eagle
C Company 101st Aviation Bn. 'Black Widow' UH-1 Phu Bai
D Company 101st Aviation Bn. 'Hawk' AH-1G Phu Bai

2nd/17th Cavalry
HQ Troop.
Saber UH-1 Eagle

A Troop
Scout Platoon Assault '10-19' OH-6 Quang Tri
Gunship Platoon Assault '20-29' AH-1G Quang Tri
Aero Rifle Platoon Ground Element Assault '30-39' Quang Tri
Aero Rifle Platoon Flight Element Assault '40-49' UH-1 Quang Tri

B Troop
Scout Platoon Banshee '10-19' OH-6 Eagle
Gunship Platoon Banshee '20-29' AH-1G Eagle
Aero Rifle Platoon: Ground Element Banshee '30-39' Eagle
Aero Rifle Platoon: Flight Element Banshee '40-49' UH-1 Eagle

C Troop.
Scout Platoon Condor '10-19' OH-6 Phu Bai
Gunship Platoon Condor '20-29' AH-1G Phu Bai
Aero Rifle Platoon: Ground Element Condor '30-39' Phu Bai
Aero Rifle Platoon: Flight Element Condor '40-49' UH-1 Phu Bai

377th Artillery
A Battery 'Gunner' UH-1H & OH-6 Eagle

4th/77th Aerial Rocket Artillery
A Battery. 'Dragon' AH-1G Phu Bai
B Battery. 'Toro' AH-1G Eagle
C Battery. 'Griffin' AH-1G Evans

326th Medical Bn. 'Dustoff' UH-1 Eagle
1st Bde. 'Dead Bone' UH-1 Evans
2nd Bde. 'Brandy' UH-1 Phu Bai
3rd Bde. 'Thunder' UH-1 Eagle

163rd Aviation Bn 'Roadrunner' UH-1 Eagle

Heavy lift
159th Aviation Bn
A Company. 'Pachyderm' CH-47 Phu Bai
B Company. 'Varsity' CH-47 Eagle
C Company. 'Playtex' CH-47 Phu Bai

478th Aviation Company 'Hurricane' CH-54 Da Nang

PEOPLE

MAJOR GENERAL OLINTO MARK BARSANTI

Of all the men who commanded the 101st Airborne Division in Vietnam, the most celebrated is Major General Olinto Mark Barsanti. In his 31-year military career, Barsanti served in the Second World War, the Korean War and Vietnam. He earned more than 60 awards, medals and commendations, including the Distinguished Service Medal, the Distinguished Service Cross, the Distinguished Flying Cross and seven Purple Hearts.

Born on 11 November 1917 to Italian immigrants, Barsanti joined the US Army and was commissioned as a Second Lieutenant, serving initially with the 2nd Infantry Division. In June 1944 he participated in Operation 'Overlord' (the Normandy landings) as commander of the 3rd Battalion, 38th Infantry. Over the next eight months of battle Major Barsanti, at 26 years of age one of the youngest battalion commanders in the army, was awarded five Purple Hearts, a Bronze Star medal and three oak leaf clusters, and the Silver Star for his leadership in combat.

Barsanti remained in Europe until April 1945, when as a lieutenant colonel he returned to the United States for medical treatment. He attended and then taught at staff college, and at the outbreak of the Korean War was serving in General Headquarters, Far East Command under General Douglas MacArthur. Lieutenant Colonel Barsanti's most notable and courageous action during the war took place on 19 and 20 October. Driving alone behind North Korean lines and subjected to repeated attacks by soldiers using automatic weapons, Barsanti successfully completed a 190-mile mission to deliver secret orders to two South Korean infantry divisions. For this he was presented the Distinguished Service Cross, the second highest military service award, on 14 December 1950.

At 33 years of age, he was commanding officer of the 9th Infantry Regiment, the army's youngest regimental commander in Korea, and added the sixth Oak Leaf Cluster to his Bronze Star and a second Oak Leaf Cluster to his Silver Star. After

COMMANDERS OF 101st AIRBORNE DIVISION

Maj Gen Thomas L. Sherbourne, Jr.	23 May 1956–23 Mar 1958
Maj Gen William C. Westmoreland	2 Apr 1958–30 June 1960
Maj Gen Ben Harrell	30 June 1960–17 July 1961
Maj Gen Charles W. G. Rich	17 July 1961–25 Feb 1963
Maj Gen Harry W. Critz	25 Feb 1963–20 Mar 1964
Maj Gen Beverly E. Powell	20 Mar 1964–28 Mar 1966
Maj Gen Ben Sternberg	28 Mar 1966–1 July 1967
Maj Gen Olinto M. Barsanti	1 July 1967–19 July 1968
Maj Gen Melvin Zais	19 July 1968–May 1969
Maj Gen John W. Wright	May 1969–25 May 1970
Maj Gen John J. Hennessey	25 May 1970–1 Feb 1971
Maj Gen Thomas M. Tarpley	1 Feb 1971–6 Apr 1972

suffering injuries in battle, Barsanti returned to Japan in August 1951 and then to the United States.

During the 1950s he served in the Far East, United States and West Germany. Colonel Barsanti was reassigned to the United States in 1957, and served in a number of capacities in Washington before returning to combat duty in July 1963 in South Korea as Assistant Division Commander for Combat Operations, 7th Infantry Division. During this time he received notification of his promotion to Brigadier General, effective 1 September 1963. This made him, at 46 years of age, one of the youngest generals in the army.

Staff positions at HQ US Army Europe, HQ V Corps and United States Army Materiel Command followed, and in May 1967 came promotion to Major General. On 1 July General Barsanti assumed command of the 101st Airborne Division at Fort Campbell. Noted as a disciplinarian, Barsanti's training programme played a major role in preparing the 101st for combat in Vietnam. At the end of the year he oversaw the uplift of the division to Vietnam, and on 13 December reported to General Westmoreland that 'the 101st Airborne Division is present for combat in Vietnam'.

In Vietnam Barsanti was a regular visitor to the frontlines, where he sometimes became engaged in combat, and to the hospitals to encourage wounded troops. His personal courage and willingness to put himself in the line of fire is attested to by the two Purple Hearts he received. During his tenure the war in Vietnam was at its most intense; through some of its toughest battles he led the 101st with great skill and courage.

In July 1968 General Barsanti turned command of the 101st in Vietnam over to General Melvin Zais. On his return he was posted to Fort Sheridan, Illinois, as Chief of Staff of the Fifth Army, and on 31 August 1971 he retired from the army on medical grounds. He died on 2 May 1973, having lost a long battle with cancer.

GENERAL MELVIN ZAIS

General Barsanti's successor in command, Melvin Zais, led the 101st Airborne in Vietnam through the tough operations in the A Shau Valley: 'Nevada Eagle', 'Somerset Plain', 'Kentucky Jumper', 'Massachusetts Striker', 'Apache Snow', and 'Lamar Plain'.

Zais was born on 8 May 1916 in Fall River, Massachusetts. After formal education, he studied political science at the University of New Hampshire. In 1937 he was commissioned a Second Lieutenant in the US Army Reserve and fought in the Second World War. After the war he attended the US Command and General Staff College, and was also a graduate of the Armed Forces Staff College and the National War College. On 1 June 1964, Zais was promoted to Brigadier General. His first command was the 1st Infantry Division (the famed Big Red One; Spearhead 6) in 1966, after which he returned to Washington as Director of Individual Training, Office, Deputy Chief of Staff for Personnel. In May 1967 he was promoted to Major General, and in July 1969 took command of the 101st Airborne Division (Airmobile). During his time as commander of the unit he proved both a worthy and able leader who is, perhaps unfairly, best remembered for the controversial decision he made at Dong Ap Bia (Hamburger Hill) to defeat the enemy at any cost. After formally handing over to John W. Wright in May 1969, Zais stayed on in Vietnam for another year as commander XXIV Corps, and was Director for Operations, J-3, Organization of the Joint Chiefs of Staff in Washington from 1970 to 1972.

His awards and decorations include the Distinguished Service Medal with three Oak Leaf Clusters, Silver Star with Oak Leaf Cluster, Legion of Merit with Two Oak Leaf Clusters, Distinguished Flying Cross with Oak Leaf Cluster, and Bronze Star Medal.

Top: General John Hennessey.

Above: General Melvin Zais.

Left: General John Cushman.

COLONEL DAVID M. HACKWORTH

Another famous – and controversial – veteran of the 101st Airborne Division is Colonel David H. Hackworth, America's most decorated living soldier, with more than 100 awards, including two Distinguished Service Crosses, 10 Silver Stars, eight Bronze Stars for Valor and eight Purple Hearts. Of the 26 years he spent in the army, seven were in combat theatres. Assigned to the 101st Airborne in January 1965, he led the 1st Battalion, 327th Infantry Regiment, into Vietnam in July and through Operations 'Highland', 'Gibraltar', 'Van Buren' and 'Hawthorn'. However, by the early 1970s he had become totally disillusioned with the way the war was being conducted and one of its most vocal public critics.

Hackworth suffered a rough childhood, and ran off to join the US Merchant Marine at the age of 14, towards the end of the Second World War. After the war, aged 15, he enlisted in the US Army and was assigned occupation duty in Trieste. The start of the Korean War found him a sergeant. Hackworth volunteered for duty and was assigned to 25th Infantry Division, winning not only a battlefield commission as a lieutenant, but medals for valour, as well as Purple Hearts. He subsequently volunteered for a second tour in Korea, serving with the 40th Infantry Division.

After the war ended, Hackworth retired from the army, and spent some time at college. Life as a civilian bored him and, using his connections, he rejoined the expanding 'cold war' US Army. Hackworth climbed the peacetime career ladder dutifully, and was a battalion commander in the 101st Airborne Division when it was sent to Vietnam in 1965. Although he led his battalion with great skill, he became rapidly soured with the conduct of the war.

Assigned to the Pentagon at the end of his one-year tour, he spent much of that assignment accompanying Brigadier General S.L.A. Marshall on a research trip. Despite mounting disillusionment, Hackworth refused to resign, feeling it was his duty as a field-grade officer to wage the campaign as best he could.

There followed a tour as commander of a training battalion of the 9th Infantry Division at Fort Lewis, Washington, which served only to convince Hackworth of the ineffectiveness of the training given to soldiers sent to Vietnam. In 1969 he returned to Vietnam, serving in a number of positions including as a senior advisor to the ARVN. His unflinching view that the US Army was not learning from its mistakes, and that the South Vietnamese ARVN officers were essentially corrupt, got him in trouble with his superior commanders. Hackworth returned home in June 1971, as the army's youngest colonel.

His disenchantment erupted in a television interview with the ABC programme *Issues and Answers*, aired on 27 June, during which he said, 'This is a bad war. ... It can't be won [and] we need to get out'. In that interview, he also said that the North Vietnamese flag would fly over Saigon in four years, a prediction that turned out to be right on target. The interview enraged senior US Army officers at the Pentagon, who ordered an investigation into his conduct in Vietnam. Although Secretary of State Robert F. Frohlke ordered this to be dropped, Hackworth was harassed and ostracised within the army, and in September retired with the rank of colonel.

After a period of self-imposed exile in Australia, Hackworth returned to the United States in the mid-1980s, where he now works as a defence analyst for the broadcast and print media, and is a vocal spokesman for veterans.

Top: General Ben Sternberg.

Above: General Thomas Tarpley.

Right: President Nixon and MoH Sgt Gordon Roberts.

MEDAL OF HONOR WINNERS

Twenty men from the division were awarded the Medal of Honor, the highest award for bravery the United States bestows on it soldiers, during the Vietnam War. Their names are given here. Posthumous awards are starred.

Sgt. 1st Class Webster Anderson
Captain Paul W. Bucha
Sp4c. Michael J. Fitzmaurice
Cpl. Frank R. Fratellenico*
1st Lt. James A. Gardner*
Staff Sgt. John G. Gertsch*
Sp4c. Peter M. Guenette*
Sp4c. Frank A. Herda
Staff Sgt. Joe R. Hooper
Sgt 1st Class Lawrence Joel
Pfc. Kenneth M. Kays
Sp4c. Joseph G. LaPointe Jr.*
Pfc. Milton A. Lee
Pfc. Carlos J. Lozada
Lt. Col. Andre C. Lucas*
Pfc. Milton L. Olive III
Sgt. Robert M. Patterson
Staff Sgt. Clifford C. Sims*
Sgt. Gordon R. Roberts
Sp4c. Dale E. Wayrynen*

MEDAL OF HONOR CITATION
ROBERTS, GORDON R.

Rank and organization: Sergeant (then Sp4c.), U.S. Army, Company B, 1st Battalion, 506th Infantry, 101st Airborne Division. Place and date: Thua Thien Province, Republic of Vietnam, 11 July 1969. Entered service at: Cincinnati, Ohio. Born: 14 June 1950, Middletown, Ohio. Citation: For conspicuous gallantry and intrepidity in action at the risk of his life above and beyond the call of duty. Sgt. Roberts distinguished himself while serving as a rifleman in Company B, during combat operations. Sgt. Roberts' platoon was maneuvering along a ridge to attack heavily fortified enemy bunker positions which had pinned down an adjoining friendly company. As the platoon approached the enemy positions, it was suddenly pinned down by heavy automatic weapons and grenade fire from camouflaged enemy fortifications atop the overlooking hill. Seeing his platoon immobilised and in danger of failing in its mission, Sgt. Roberts crawled rapidly toward the closest enemy bunker. With complete disregard for his safety, he leaped to his feet and charged the bunker, firing as he ran. Despite the intense enemy fire directed at him, Sgt. Roberts silenced the 2-man bunker. Without hesitation, Sgt. Roberts continued his 1-man assault on a second bunker. As he neared the second bunker, a burst of enemy fire knocked his rifle from his hands. Sgt. Roberts picked up a rifle dropped by a comrade and continued his assault, silencing the bunker. He continued his charge against a third bunker and destroyed it with well-thrown hand grenades. Although Sgt. Roberts was now cut off from his platoon, he continued his assault against a fourth enemy emplacement. He fought through a heavy hail of fire to join elements of the adjoining company which had been pinned down by the enemy fire. Although continually exposed to hostile fire, he assisted in moving wounded personnel from exposed positions on the hilltop to an evacuation area before returning to his unit. By his gallant and selfless actions, Sgt. Roberts contributed directly to saving the lives of his comrades and served as an inspiration to his fellow soldiers in the defeat of the enemy force. Sgt. Roberts' extraordinary heroism in action at the risk of his life were in keeping with the highest traditions of the military service and reflect great credit upon himself, his unit, and the U.S. Army.

ASSESSMENT

The 101st Airborne was the last army division to leave the Vietnam war zone, after almost seven years in combat. For the greater part of this time the division fought in I Corps, scene of most of the toughest fighting and where most casualties occurred. 4,011 men were killed and another 18,259 wounded. The 1st Brigade spent a total of about 2,200 days in combat, while the full Division (including the 2nd and 3rd Brigades spent a total of 1,573 days.

The 101st Airborne Division came to war in Vietnam with a very illustrious history and many laurels. But past glories do not win battles. It is to the credit of the division that it did not rest on its laurels, instead re-igniting the legendary airborne *esprit de corps* within the ranks to fight difficult battles in trying circumstances in a war that many believe the United States could not win. Nevertheless, despite the misgivings that many of the men must have had, countless acts of courage have been documented and undoubtedly many more went unrecorded. Statistics can never tell the full picture, but one worth noting is that 17 Medals of Honor were awarded to 101st Airborne troops during the Vietnam War. Another statistic that speaks volumes about the character of these men is that almost 2,000, mostly in infantry battalions, extended their Vietnam tours by six months.

One measure of any unit is the regard in which it is held by its enemy. According to divisional lore, many enemy commanders warned their men to avoid the 'Chicken Men' at all costs, because any engagement with them would surely be lost. In the end, perhaps the final word should go to one of their number. In his farewell to the 101st Division, Barsanti stated: "I have pushed hard and demanded much, always knowing what the results would be – success and victory. During the last six months you have established records that other units have not surpassed in much longer periods of time. This is a tribute to your dedication, 'will to win,' and discipline as an airborne division."

UNIT CITATIONS

Republic of Vietnam Cross of Gallantry with Palm for Vietnam 1968-1969
Republic of Vietnam Cross of Gallantry with Palm for Vietnam 1971
Republic of Vietnam Civil Action Honor Medal, First Class for Vietnam 1968-1970

Presidential Unit Citation (Army), Streamer embroidered Dak To, Vietnam 1966
Presidential Unit Citation (Army), Streamer embroidered Dong Ap Bia Mountain

Valorous Unit Award, Streamer embroidered Tuy Hoa
Valorous Unit Award, Streamer embroidered Thua Thien
Valorous Unit Award, Streamer embroidered Thua Thien

Meritorious Unit Commendation (Army), Streamer embroidered Vietnam 1965-1966
Meritorious Unit Commendation (Army), Streamer embroidered Vietnam 1968
Meritorious Unit Commendation (Army), Streamer embroidered Vietnam 1968-1969

POSTWAR

Today, the 101st Airborne (Air Assault) is the US Army's and the world's only air assault division, and continues to develop and exploit the doctrine of air assault.

In January 1991, during the first Gulf War, the 101st Airborne made the deepest and largest combat air assault in history, when 2,000 men, 50 transport vehicles, artillery, and tons of fuel and ammunition were airlifted 50 miles into Iraq. Remarkable, the division suffered no soldiers killed in action, and captured thousands of enemy prisoners of war. Since that time its soldiers have supported humanitarian relief efforts in Rwanda and Somalia, and more recently supplied peacekeepers to Haiti and Bosnia. When the US 'War on Terror' began after the events of 11 September, elements from the 101st went into Afghanistan as part of Operation 'Anaconda' to drive the Taliban regime from power and the al Qaeda organization out of the country. At the end of February 2003, the division deployed to Kuwait and took part in the subsequent invasion of Iraq. It has since been occupied on occupation duties in that country under Operation 'Enduring Freedom'.

Left: SP4 Dale Wayrynen won his Medal of Honor posthumously. On 18 May 1967, during combat operations near Duc Pho, his platoon came face to face with the enemy and during the fighting, a live enemy grenade landed in the centre of the tightly grouped Americans. Wayrynen threw himself on the grenade at the moment it exploded.

Below: A CH-47E Chinook helicopter comes in for a landing at Udairi air base in Kuwait as a UH-60 Black Hawk waits for clearance to move onto the runway on 29 March 2003. All the aircraft are from the 101st Airborne Division (Air Assault) based at Fort Campbell, and deployed in support of Operation 'Iraqi Freedom'.

REFERENCE

WEBSITES

UNIT WEBSITES/HISTORIES

http://www.army.mil/cmh-pg/matrix/Matrix.htm
Details of 101st insignia, commanders and history.

http://screamingeagles-327thvietnam.com/
101st Airborne, 327th Infantry Regiment Vietnam Veterans site. Good information on the battles fought by this unit plus good photographs of fire bases.

http://www.b2501airborne.com/
Company B, 2nd Battalion, 501st Infantry website.

http://www.currahee.org/
3rd Battalion, 506th Airborne Infantry, 1st Brigade, 101st Airborne Division.

http://www.a101avn.org/
101st Aviation Battalion website.

Unit histories

http://www.campbell.army.mil/division.htm
Details units currently stationed at Fort Campbell, including those of 101st Airborne.

http://101_lha.tripod.com/101st_lha/id6.html
History of 101st Airborne in Vietnam.

http://www.angelfire.com/rebellion/101abndivvietvets/page15history101.html
History of 101st Airborne in Vietnam.

http://www.screamingeaglesthroughtime.com/id119.html
Month by month diary of actions.

http://screamingeagles-327thvietnam.com/second/trung_luong/20_jun.htm
A very detailed account of the Battle for Trung Luong, fought by the 2nd Battalion of the 327th Regiment, by Colonel (Ret.) Tom Furgeson.

GENERAL HISTORY

http://www.vietnamwar.com/
Good general background to the war.

http://members.aol.com/veterans/warlib6v.htm
Comprehensive page of links to Vietnam resources.

http://www.cc.gatech.edu/fac/Thomas.Pilsch/Vietnam.html
Another excellent page of links.

http://www.screamingeagle.org
101st Airborne Division Association, the Screaming Eagles Veterans' Website.

MISCELLANEOUS

http://www.army.mil/cmh-pg/
Homepage of the US Army Center for Military History.

http://www.vietnamtripledeuce.org/PresidentialUnitCitation.pdf
Presidential citation for Operation 'Hawthorne'.

http://vietnamresearch.com/unif/
Excellent table showing relevant US Army rank insignia.

http://www.quanonline.com/military/military_reference/american/american.html
Information on clothing and insignia.

http://www.3rdmarines.net/Vietnam_Operations_by_Name.htm
Brief details of US military operations in Vietnam (from 1966).

http://www.ehistory.com/vietnam/pdf/101airborne.pdf
Official post-battle report form, Dong Ap Bia (Hamburger Hill).

The online archive of the Vietnam Project at Texas Tech University is also an extensive resource for reference works published by the US Government and US Army.

BIBLIOGRAPHY

BOOKS AND ARTICLES

Bowman, John S. (ed.): *The Vietnam War – An Almanac*, World Almanac Publications, 1985. The bulk of the volume is a detailed chronology.

Burns, Richard R.: *Pathfinder – First In, Last Out*, Ballantine, 2002.
Burns was in the Pathfinder detachment, Headquarters Company, 101st Aviation Battalion from December 1967 to December 1968.

Clodfelter, Michael: *Mad Minutes and Vietnam Months*, Zebra Books, 1989.
Clodfelter served in Vietnam with the 101st Airborne from July 1965 to December 1966.

Chinnery, Philip D.: *Vietnam – The Helicopter War*, Naval Institute Press, 1991.

Far Right: Three soldiers from the 101st Airborne Division, one armed with a 5.56mm Colt M4 carbine equipped with the Knights Armament Company (KAC) Modular Weapon System (MWS), observe movement from atop a fortified bunker position at the Kandahar, International Airport, Afghanistan, during Operation Enduring Freedom, January 2002.

Below Left and Right: The six-colour 'chocolate chip' desert camouflage uniform was introduced in the late 1970s following the creation of the Rapid Deployment Force. This trooper of the 101st Airborne Division (Air Assault) is cleaning his M16A2 5.56mm assault rifle at the outsell of Operation 'Desert Storm' in February 1991 with the Kevlar PASGT 'Fritz' helmet on his head that replaced the venerable steel M1 helmet of World War II and the Vietnam era. As part of US XVIII Airborne Corps, the 101st Airborne Division (Air Assault) was deployed to the western edge of the Coalition Forces as the flank protection for the major assault of the armoured and mechanised divisions of US VII Corps. Using its awesome aviation assets, the division air assaulted deep into Iraq as far as the Euphrates river valley. Here (left), AH-64A Apache attack helicopters and their companion OH-58D Kiowa observation helicopters wait for their next mission during Operation 'Desert Storm'.

Gadd, Charles: *Line Doggie – Foot Soldier in Vietnam*; Presidio, 1987.
Gadd served a one-year tour with the 1st Battalion, 501st Infantry, starting in December 1967.

Grant, William T.: *Wings of the Eagle – A Kingsmen's Story*; Ivy, 1994.

Gregory, Barry: *Vietnam Helicopter Handbook*; Patrick Stephens, 1988.

Hackworth, Col. David H. and Sherman, Julie: *About Face – The Odyssey of an American Warrior*; Simon & Schuster, 1989.

Kelly, Michael P.: *Where We Were in Vietnam – A Comprehensive Guide to the Firebases, Military Installations and Naval Vessels of the Vietnam War, 1945–1975*; Hellgate, 2002.

Lepore, Herbert P.: 'The Coming of Age –The Role of the Helicopter in the Vietnam War'; *Army History*, No. 29, Winter, 1994, pp. 29–36.

Nolan, Keith William: *Ripcord – Screaming Eagles under Siege, Vietnam 1970*; Presidio Press, 2000.

Rosser-Owen, David: *Vietnam Weapons Handbook*; Patrick Stephens, 1986
Stanton, Shelby L.: *Vietnam Order of Battle*; US News Books, 1981.
Foreword by General William C. Westmoreland. A vital reference work listing US units, with dates and locations of Vietnam service, etc.

Tucker, Spencer C (ed.): *The Encyclopedia of the Vietnam War – A Political, Social and Military History*; OUP, 1998.

MAGAZINES AND PERIODICALS
In Combat, Marshall Cavendish Magazine Collection.
The Vietnam Experience, Orbis Magazine Collection.

MONUMENTS

In June 2004 a new monument was unveiled at Fort Campbell to honour the soldiers who have served in the 101st Airborne Division throughout its history.

The monument, directly in front of the division headquarters building, is a large, jet-black granite obelisk with panels that depict the division's storied history: in the Second World War, the Vietnam conflict, Operation 'Desert Storm' and recent operations including Operations 'Enduring Freedom' and 'Iraqi Freedom'.

INDEX